This is the Church that God Built

A History of Crossway Church

Revd Peter Stevenson

Onwards and Upwards Publishers

3 Radfords Turf, Cranbrook, Exeter,
EX5 7DX, United Kingdom.
www.onwardsandupwards.org

First edition, published in the United Kingdom by Onwards and Upwards Publishers (2018).

ISBN: 978-1-78815-725-4
Typeface: Sabon LT
Graphic design: LM Graphic Design

Printed in the United Kingdom.

Endorsements

The story of any church cannot be told in isolation from the community in which it is set, and Crossway is no exception here. Through the commitment and faith of many, the book bears witness to the ways in which the church was founded as a response to *The Bitter Cry* report of 1883. Throughout the 20th Century and into the 21st, the church has gone on serving the Elephant and Castle community in the aftermath of two world wars and in the present day meeting the challenges of a constantly changing multi-ethnic capital city. It is clear that Crossway has remained an ever-present expression of Christian Hope that goes far beyond the walls of the three buildings that it has called home.

I have no doubt that God is already at work in writing the next chapter in the story of His church called Crossway URC, and if past history is anything to go by, it won't be the last!

Revd David Salsbury
URC Minister in Dyseth;
Training Officer for North Wales; and
Director of *Stepwise,* the URC lay training programme

Peter Stevenson has written a serious history in his characteristically bright and breezy style. He is not afraid to cover the earlier history of his church but includes here conversation with present and former members. This is a welcome addition to the history of south London. His church has played and continues to play a significant role in the life of the community.

Revd Dr Alan Argent
Minister of Brixton Congregation Church;
Editor of the Congregational History Society Magazine; and
Research Fellow at Dr Williams's Library, London

About the Author

Peter Stevenson was ordained in 2000, moving to London in 2009 as a Special Category Minister within the United Reformed Church, and was encouraged to build a new church, a congregation and a community in the Elephant and Castle area. He is married with two children.

Peter was educated in Cambridge and Princeton USA and holds both a Bachelor of Theology and a Doctor of Ministry. He regularly broadcasts on BBC Radio London.

Acknowledgements

We are grateful to:

- *David Powell* at Dr Williams's Library for his help in investigating the materials held there;
- *Maggie Gray* for interrogating the very rough first draft produced by Revd Peter Stevenson;
- *Luke Jeffery* of Onwards and Upwards Publishers for making the final edit and producing a wonderful book;
- *Crossway United Reformed Church* for funding the project; and
- *you,* the reader, for investing your time and energy in order to learn how 'This is the Church that God Built'.

This is the Church that God Built

This book is dedicated to God to
whom all glory and honour is due.

We also thank the church
members both past and present
for keeping the faith alive and
sharing their faith with many.

This is the Church that God Built

Contents

This is the Church that God Built

Introduction

IN THE GREAT SCHEME OF THINGS, CROSSWAY UNITED Reformed Church is a minnow in an ocean of churches, hardly worth a mention when compared with cathedrals, abbeys and citadels around the world. But to those who have been part of the story of the church, it is of vital importance. It is the place where memories have been forged and friendships made; a place where tears have been shed and laughter shared; it has been a spiritual home.

The United Reformed Church (URC) was born when the Presbyterian Church of England and the Congregational Church of England and Wales came together on 21 June 1972. The URC subsequently united with the Re-formed Association of the Churches of Christ in 1981 and the Congregational Union of Scotland in 2000. Crossway itself dates back further. It was previously part of the London Congregational Union (LCU), and its links with the former Pilgrim Fathers' Memorial Church in Great Dover Street tie it in to an even longer history of reformist Christianity in the south London area. The church has served the community of the Elephant and Castle from three different buildings over the years. The purpose of this book is to trace some of its history against the wider context of urban ministry.

The latest chapter of Crossway's story was completed in February 2017, when the church was relocated into a new building following the demolition and redevelopment of the Heygate Estate. The move was overseen by Revd Peter Stevenson, who is also the author of this book and minister of the church at the time of writing. Revd Stevenson was called to the pastorate as a Special Category Minister in 2009 for an initial period of five years that was extended by a further five years in 2014. His task was to build the church, build the congregation and build the community.

The names of church ministers are readily available, but the stories of other church members and worshippers are less easy to find. Many of Crossway's documents have been lost during its various relocations. This book attempts to act as a more lasting record of a special place where God has resided and poured out His love with abundant grace. It aims to provide readers who have an interest in the present church with an opportunity to hear from those who attended in the past. Elephant and Castle has long had a reputation of being 'down-at-heel', and people from outside the neighbourhood have offered help and encouragement over the years. Their stories are told here, too.

In 2018, the Crossway archive consisted of minutes books from December 1957 to Easter 1963, January 1983 to October 1985, and February 1996 to date; *Crossway Chronicle* editions from January 1958 to September 1964; a Roll of Church Members register from 1933 to 1952; and two folders of sundry correspondence and documents. Additional information was gathered during the author's visits to Dr Williams's Library (mainly Congregational Union yearbooks); the London Metropolitan Archives (marriage certificate records); and John Harvard Library, Borough High Street. Interviews with a number of former ministers and people connected with the church supplemented these materials in the formulation of the book, and many of them are quoted at length in these pages. Wherever possible, primary source materials have been used and expanded upon, so that the first-hand accounts of the people who were involved in the church and community sit at the heart of the narrative. These have been edited lightly where required for readability, but are otherwise presented as found.

The purpose of this book is to explore who built the church. It is not a simple task. The physical labour that went into constructing the existing building can be credited to Martin Burfield and Martin Burke *et al.* of Heritage Brickwork. But they could not have laid a single brick if Mandip, Awinder and Jasvir Singh had not poured the concrete foundations, and they could not have done that without Dorin Condranschi doing the preparatory steel fixings. None of the afore-mentioned could be on site if Neal Mansukh and Mike Saxton had not allowed them to work there after checking their accreditation and completing their inductions. Before the site managers took the lead, architects, quantity surveyors, council officers and officials were involved in approving the designs, completing the costing and setting budgetary constraints. The URC Southern Synod Trust officer Guy Morfett had to ensure the church was value for money. Wider church councils had to affirm that the redevelopment was *'the right thing to do'*. Crossway church members needed to pass resolutions and give authority to proceed.

So, who did build the church? As this book's title suggests, this is the church that God built, but it is also the story of the people He involved.

CHAPTER ONE

Constant Regeneration

THE POPULAR TV SERIES *DOCTOR WHO* MAY TELL US SOME-thing about regeneration. As the Wikipedia page for the drama, in which the lead character is routinely 'reincarnated' in a new body, explains:

> *The transition from one actor to another is written into the plot of the show with the concept of regeneration into a new incarnation – an idea introduced in 1966 to allow the show to continue after the departure of original lead William Hartnell who was becoming very ill at the time. The concept is that this is a Time Lord trait through which the character of the Doctor takes on a new body and personality to recover from a severe injury or anything that would otherwise kill a normal person. Each actor's portrayal differs, but all represent stages in the life of the same character and form a single narrative. The time-travelling feature of the plot means that different incarnations of the Doctor occasionally meet.[1]*

Crossway has certainly experienced a number of regenerations and morphed over time into the place it is today. Is it possible to look into the past to discover the DNA of the church and establish why God has willed its presence in the Elephant and Castle? To what extent does Crossway retain the same character despite its numerous different portrayals?

The Crossway story has no definite starting point and certainly no ending, so all we can do is provide a snapshot of some of the people involved, the area it has served and the impact it has had.

---

[1] 'Doctor Who', Wikipedia, accessed 29 December 2017, *https://en.wikipedia.org/wiki/Doctor_Who.*

The beginning of Crossway

The first definite 'incarnation' of the church was as the 'South London Mission, Crossway', which opened on 8 November 1905 with a two-and-a-half-hour ceremony that was attended by 1,000 people.

The *London Congregational Yearbook* of 1906 suggests that the church actually dates back earlier, to 1855. It includes a tantalising reference to 'Murphey's Chapel', which was possibly the forerunner to Crossway. *The Surman Index of Congregational Ministers* records George Fuller as serving Murphy Memorial, New Kent Road, London, Middlesex, between the years 1896 and 1904, having served previously in Ontario from 1883 to 1896.[2] An earlier reference in the same publication suggests that David Bayne Morris ministered in New Kent Road in 1870 before being ordained into the Church of England and becoming a missionary in Calcutta (Kolkata), India.

It is possible that Crossway was opened as a new entity on the site of the Murphy Memorial Hall, which was described as *'an institution which, from lack of efficient man, had hitherto failed to meet with that measure of prosperity which is rightly expected of a centre of relevant work'.[3]*

A Bitter Cry: Crossway in context

Church leaders of Victorian and Edwardian London were greatly influenced by a report entitled *The Bitter Cry of Outcast London: An Inquiry into the Condition of the Abject Poor,* which was written by Andrew Mearns (secretary of the London Congregational Union) and William C. Preston and first published in 1883. It paints an uncomfortable picture of the city and the Church's response to the social deprivation of the time:

> *Whilst we have been building our churches and solacing ourselves with our religion and dreaming that the millennium was coming, the poor have been growing poorer, the wretched more miserable, and the immoral more corrupt; the gulf has been daily widening which separates the lowest classes of the*

---

[2] The Surman Index Online, accessed 29 December 2017, *https://surman.english.qmul.ac.uk.*

[3] Ernest H. Jeffs, 'A Few Words ... Inauguration Day', 1905, CH.A.6 (7), Dr Williams's Library, London.

community from our churches and chapels, and from all decency and civilisation. It is easy to bring an array of facts which seem to point to the opposite conclusion – to speak of the noble army of men and women who penetrate the vilest haunts, carrying with them the blessings of the gospel; of the encouraging reports published by Missions, Reformatories, Refuges, Temperance Societies; of Theatre Services, Midnight Meetings and Special Missions. But what does it all amount to? We are simply living in a fool's paradise if we suppose that all these agencies combined are doing a thousandth part of what needs to be done, a hundredth part of what could be done by the Church of Christ.[4]

The report speaks of the miserable living conditions suffered by the urban poor and the widespread non-attendance at worship, suggesting that immorality is an outcome of poverty. The authors argue that something needs to be done, *'for this pitiable outcast population must be evident to all who have read these particulars as to their condition'.[5]* The report ends with a challenge:

Will you venture to come with us and see for yourselves the ghastly reality? Others, looking on, will believe, and pity, and despair. But another vision will be seen by many, and in this lies our hope – a vision of Him who had 'compassion upon the multitude because they were as sheep having no shepherd,' looking with Divine pity in His eyes, over this outcast London, and then turning to the consecrated host of His Church with the appeal, 'Whom shall we send and who will go for us?'[6]

Many denominations took seriously the report and sought to respond. John D. Beasley, a well-known local historian, has written a number of books on the London Borough of Southwark and contributed over 150 local history articles to the South London Press. He has compiled the archive of the Bermondsey Methodist Church under the title

4 Revd Andrew Mearns and William C. Preston, *The Bitter Cry of Outcast London: An Inquiry into the Condition of the Abject Poor*, (London: James Clarke & Co., 1883), accessed 29 December 2017, *http://www.attackingthedevil.co.uk/related/outcast.php.*
5 *Ibid.*
6 *Ibid.*

The Bitter Cry Heard and Heeded in which he refers to its impact, concluding:

> *In South London the emotional response slowly led to practical action. Six years after the pamphlet was published, Wesleyan Methodists took a major step forward in the Long Lane area of Bermondsey. The birth of the South London Mission demonstrated that the bitter cry of needy people was heard and heeded.*[7]

The Bermondsey church was established in 1885, first as the London Wesleyan Methodist Mission before being renamed the South London Mission in 1889. When Crossway was conceived in 1905, it became known as the London Congregational Union's South London Mission to avoid confusion between the two places. Before long, it had been renamed Crossway Central Mission Church. Crossway, like the Bermondsey church, was formed in part in response to *The Bitter Cry* report.

In Charles Booth's famous 'Maps Descriptive of London Poverty' (part of his *Inquiry into Life and Labour in London; 1886-1903)*, the Elephant and Castle is classed as a place of poor to very poor people.[8] The Ordnance Survey Map of 1896 indicates the density of housing in the area. In 1905 it was reported that 46 per cent of local households lived in a state of poverty with income of less than £1 per week, while the average number of people living in a single home was ten (the London average at the time was five).[9] At the time, around one in six local people attended a place of worship.

London Congregational Union's response to *The Bitter Cry*

Until 1831, congregational and independent churches had no central organisation, though a number of county unions had been formed. That year, the Congregational Union of England and Wales was founded, remaining in existence until its constituent churches formed themselves into the Congregational Church in England and Wales in 1966. The

---

[7] John D. Beasley, *The Bitter Cry Heard and Heeded* (London: South London Mission, c.1989), p. 13.
[8] Charles Booth, *Map Descriptive of London Poverty*, 1898-99, *https://booth.lse.ac.uk/learn-more/download-maps/sheet9.*
[9] 'A Few Words', *op cit.*

London Congregational Union (LCU) was formed in 1873. At the turn of the century, influenced by *The Bitter Cry* – which was, after all, co-authored by one of their own – the LCU sought to open Mission Centres to serve the urban poor.

Crossway, 1905.

Two Central Missions were opened by the LCU before Crossway – one at Claremont Church in Pentonville (1902) and another at Whitefield, Tottenham Court Road (1903). These were intended to bring to the *'forefront the redemptive power of the Christian gospel'.*[10] It was soon decided that a third Central Mission should be established in south London. An undated article in Dr Williams's Library records that:

> *The centre of the Mission is the hall in the New Kent Road which was erected to the memory of George Mollett Murphy (1823-87), a Temperance evangelist who served Borough Road Congregational Church from 1866 to his death, and was*

---

[10] 'Why, What and Where', printed matter, undated, CH.Lo.P.81, Dr Williams's Library archive, London.

once associated with Dr Newman Hall at Surrey Chapel, who made an abiding impression on the district 20 years ago.[11]

The article goes on to say, *'Though modern, the Murphy Memorial Hall was not modern enough for the London Union's idea of an up-to-date central mission.'*[12] Thanks in part to the generosity of Mr W.H. Brown, a banker from Woodford, the work to redevelop the halls was undertaken – but not before the churches of the Metropolitan Kent and Metropolitan Surrey unions pledged £1,000 per annum to ensure that the work of the mission could be sustained. At the time, the two unions comprised 93 congregations. The author(s) of the article explained that *'[t]he new Central Mission is to be an active rival of the public house'*, adding that *'brightness, lightness and cleanliness are the three watchwords of the new [centre]'.*[13] Speaking at the inaugural service, Revd F.B. Meyer reflected on the new building, remarking that the mission was *'giving the poor people the precious ointment [referring to Jesus] in an alabaster box'* and adding, *'I like your box very much. There's nothing cheap or shoddy about the Mission Hall now, it is spacious, bright and light.'*[14]

The Central Mission would need a superintendent. So it was that Revd Herbert Kenward from Norwich was called. The 32-year-old had displayed driving energy following his appointment to Magdalen Road Church after graduating from Nottingham College. He had a remarkable capacity to organise and his enthusiasm was contagious.

By 1910 Revd Kenward had been joined by Ernest Hanson as assistant superintendent, Douglas Young as treasurer and T. Knight Ball as financial secretary. Membership of the church had reached 255, and the 68th London Boys' Brigade Company had been established. A map from John H. Taylor's *L.C.U. Story, 1873-1972* records the number of congregational churches located in the triangle defined by Old Kent Road, Walworth Road and Albany Road as nine.[15]

11 'The South London Central Mission', printed matter, undated, CH.A.6(8), Dr Williams's Library, London.
12 *Ibid.*
13 *Ibid.*
14 *Ibid.*
15 John H. Taylor, *L.C.U. Story, 1873-1972* (London: Richard J. Hall, 1972).

Revd Herbert Kenward.

These developments are recorded in a church report entitled 'Snap Shots by Pen and Camera', produced by Ernest H. Jeffs in 1911. Mr Jeffs was a layman who chronicled the first ten years of Crossway Central Mission Church, producing informative and thorough annual reports. He went on to edit *The Christian World* from 1936 and was author of books on mission and the church. This report gives an idea of what was going on day by day at the young Crossway. The weekly timetable is worth reproducing here in full:

Mondays	*2:30*	*Women's Club – blouse making*
	7:30	*Benefit Society*
	7:30	*Christmas Club*
	8:00	*Women's meeting*
	8:15	*Bible class*
	8:30	*Men's gymnasium*
Tuesdays	*8:00*	*Basket work class for juniors*
	8:00	*Brass band practice*
	8:00	*Fancy work class*
	8:15	*Southwark Parliament*

Wednesdays	2:30	Women's club
	3:30	Women's bible class
	6:30	Guild of play
	7:00	Bugle band practice
	8:00	Junior girls' club
	8:00	Boys' Brigade drill
	8:00	Basket work class for seniors
	8:00	Choir practice
	8:30	Sing song
	8:30	Girls drill class
	8:30	Chess and draughts club
	9:00	Male voice choir practice
Thursdays	6:45	Band of Hope
	7:00	Poor man's lawyer
	8:00	Boys Brigade gymnasium
	8:00	Building Society
	8:15	People's service
Fridays	2:00	Mothers welcome
	2:30	Women's club
	3:00	Lecture for women
	6:30	Guild of play
	7:45	Junior girls drill class (i)
	8:00	Dress making classes
	8:00	Primary training class
	8:45	Junior girls drill class (ii)
Saturdays	3:00	Rambling, football and cycling clubs
	5:30	Children's cinematography
	6:00	Slate club
	6:00	Coal club
	6:00	Christmas club
	8:00	Popular concert and cinematography

But Sunday was the busiest day of all:

Sundays		
	9:00	Adult school
	10:15	Boys Brigade bible class
	10:15	Junior school
	11:00	Worship
	3:00	Sunday school
	3:30	Brotherhood
	3:30	Young women meeting
	4:30	Tea
	6:00	Children's evening mission
	6:40	Musical service
	7:00	People's service
	8:15	Open-air service

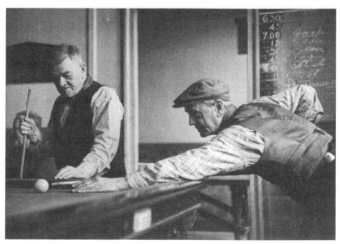

The range of events and activities offered by Crossway each week illustrates how the church was used to develop people and encourage them to make the most of what they had. Images from the time show how the building functioned as much more than a place of worship. It was a social club where the men and women could find recreation and support.

Much of this was down to the vision of Revd Kenward – a remarkable minister, pastor, priest, building manager, visionary and many other things. Although he was not able to achieve everything he set out to do, he was able to develop the site into an impressive suite of spaces that could serve the community. When Crossway's work outgrew the space available he simply went about adding another room. He was a tireless fundraiser and found ways to supply whatever he saw was needed.

An image from 'Snap Shots' indicating the vision Revd Kenward had for the building and although he was not able to achieve everything he set out to do, he managed to develop the site into an impressive suite of rooms and spaces able to respond to the needs of the community.

Crossway after the wars

The original building served Crossway well for many years. During the Second World War it escaped the worst of the London Blitz that obliterated much of the area. One young resident of the time later recalled:

> *The Blitz grew in intensity. Schools only opened an hour a day, if at all. We rarely managed to get there before the sirens sent*

us scurrying for shelter. No sauntering along nonchalantly as if nothing was amiss, we put our heads down and RAN.

The raids were almost continuous now, starting about six in the evenings and lasting until about six in the morning. Between raids we might get about an hour's respite, then the bombing started again.[16]

Like much of London after the war, the area around Crossway needed substantial reconstruction. Southwark Council decided to clear the slum dwellings in the process and create an urban utopia in its place. The 'View from the Mirror' website, a London cabbie's blog which charts the history of parts of London, reflects that,

By far the largest post-war project to grace the Elephant and Castle was the vast Heygate Estate, which was completed in 1974 and provided homes for 3,000 people.[17]

Crossway was relocated 50 yards down the New Kent Road toward the Bricklayers Arms to accommodate the new development. The construction of the Heygate Estate, and of the second Crossway building with it, took years to complete, and displaced most of the congregation in the process.

Designed by Tim Tinker, the Heygate Estate was very much a product of its time; a huge housing scheme conjured on an incredibly ambitious scale, and designed with the best of intentions in mind. Aiming to make the estate an oasis of calm away from Elephant's characteristic roar of traffic, Tim Tinker placed the tallest of the tower blocks around the perimeter, encircling and shielding smaller accommodation and areas of greenery within the middle.[18]

---

[16] Bill Cole, 'The Blitz in the Elephant and Castle, London and my family's removal to Feltham, Middlesex after being bombed out', Hounslow Local Studies, contributed to the BBC 22 October 2005, accessed 29 December 2017,
http://www.bbc.co.uk/history/ww2peopleswar/stories/67/a6287367.shtml.

[17] 'A History of the Elephant and Castle (Part 2)', View from the Mirror, 26 October 2012, accessed 29 December.

[18] *Ibid.*

In keeping with the architecture of the estate, the new church was constructed in concrete with five flat roofs which proved difficult to maintain. The building was officially opened on Saturday 25 January 1975, although images from the time show evidence of continued building works.

The picture above was taken before a London plane tree was planted in front of the building that would eventually hide the entrance, making the church largely anonymous. Few minutes or records exist from this time as many of them were stolen during a break-in (one wonders why anyone wanted them?) But a letter from the serving minister Revd Ralph Essex survives from August 1975:

> *We walked over to Crossway where the dedication of the new building was conducted jointly by our own Moderator, Revd. Vernon Lowis, the Bishop (Rt Revd David Sheppard) and Revd Douglas Bale Chairman of Bromley District, U.R.C. This service took place in the Church with everybody standing because the closed circuit television which had been ordered hadn't come. (The firm have since apologised and made amends with a cheque for £50.) We then went down to the*

hall where most people got a seat. The sermon was preached by Rt Revd Arthur MacArthur.[19]

The congregation had been out of their own building for well over three years and the evacuation of the old estates to enable the Heygate to be built left *'only three members fit enough to take an active part in the life of the church'.[20]* There was a huge and difficult rebuilding task ahead of the clergy team. Since the move into the New Kent Road building, membership has hovered at around 20 while the average congregation size for the main Sunday morning service has declined reaching a low of just 15 in 2016. Ministers have come and gone, often very quickly: between 1975 and 2018 Crossway has had 11 different leaders.

The new, new Crossway

The concrete dream fast became a nightmare, and as early as 1996 Southwark Council began to talk about regenerating the area again. The cost of bringing the existing properties on the Heygate Estate in line with new health and safety requirements proved uneconomic and it was decided that the estate must be demolished. Crossway was in danger of becoming homeless again!

As the situation developed, the *Southwark News* ran an article on Thursday 29 July 2010 under the title 'Three town halls could be put up for sale'[21]. Towards the end of the piece the reporter mentions a possible new venue for Crossway, in Walworth's old town hall:

> *The building in Walworth, which houses the Cuming Museum and a Library, could solve a thorny issue with Crossway Church, which owns the freehold on the Heygate Estate. One option is a land swap where the church would move to the town hall in exchange for giving up its existing building and a flat it owns on the neighbouring estate.*

The church had not been approached about this offer and its leadership was surprised to see Crossway described as a *'thorny issue'.* In

---

[19] Correspondence from Revd Ralph Essex, August 1975, Crossway United Reformed Church archives.

[20] Visitation report, summer 1976, Crossway United Reformed Church archives.

[21] 'Three Town Halls could be put up for Sale', *Southwark News,* Thursday 29 July 2010. Cutting from personal diary of Revd Stevenson.

response Revd Stevenson was interviewed by the newspaper and a follow-up article appeared the next week.[22] A few days after that, the Head of Regeneration at Southwark Council approached the church and formally offered the redundant Walworth Town Hall. After protracted negotiations, the Synod Trust decided that the site was too large an undertaking and the URC pulled out on 20 September 2011. Naturally, the people of Crossway were disappointed, but six months later the council offered another opportunity, to redevelop the former Castle Day Centre on Hampton Street that had remained empty for the past two years.

Negotiations took a long time, with worries about costs and long-term sustainability causing significant delays and dilemmas. Eventually everything settled down and pre-construction (demolition to you and me) started on 16 November 2015, with a completion date set for 5 December 2016 – it did not happen.

The last service of the 1975 building went ahead on 31 December 2016 and was shared by five of the congregations that were using the church at the time. The promised completion date was missed, and the people of Crossway again found themselves without a building. A service was held at the incomplete Hampton Street building on Christmas Eve, but because it had to be held outside the front doors it was entitled 'No room at the Inn'.

There were three opening services in total: one for the members; one for the Synod; and the Civic Opening on 26 April 2017, which had many local and church leaders in attendance. The reception included a spread of chicory boats, filo pastry cups, blinis, chocolate mousse and Oreo cheesecake 'shooters', but no alcohol as the Church Meeting council wished to observe the same principles of temperance on which the early church was founded.

Crossway today

One year on, the Crossway building hosts ten congregations in addition to its own, three day centres, three dance schools, and countless other groups and users. The 'home' congregation is growing and there is

---

[22] John Prendergast, response to 'Three Town Halls could be put up for Sale', *Southwark News,* Thursday 5 August 2010.

much excitement about the future ministry that will be possible from the new purpose-built church.

The completion of the new building was the inspiration for this book. Reflecting on how many people were involved in constructing the new church led to the idea of telling the full story of Crossway from its remaining archives. A list of 500 people who were involved in the physical construction of the current building is included as an appendix, but when we say 'This is the Church that God Built', we should consider the longer story of how various people and ideas came together over the decades. It is this historic and ongoing community that ensures that God's will is done, and that Crossway can enter into the next 100 years of service to the community in the Elephant and Castle.

Chapter Two

The Pilgrim Fathers

NEITHER CROSSWAY, NOW THE UNITED REFORMED CHURCH (URC), nor the London Congregational Union (LCU) can claim direct connection with the Pilgrim Fathers, but they are all firmly placed within the reformed tradition which has strong historical links to Southwark. Crossway's most tangible link to the famous religious dissenters was made in the 20th century when the leadership of the Pilgrim Fathers' Memorial Church on Great Dover Street could no longer manage the building and passed ownership over to Crossway. It is worth looking back over the long history of reformist religion in the area in order to better understand these loose but longstanding connections.

The *Mayflower* and the New World

In the summer of 1620, around 65 pilgrims boarded the *Mayflower*, skippered by Captain Jones, and left port at Rotherhithe to meet with the *Speedwell* at Southampton before they both set sail for America. The *Speedwell* sprang a leak, forcing them to turn back twice before the *Mayflower* took on her passengers and finally departed Plymouth on 6 September 1620 with just over 100 pilgrims on board. Land was sighted on 9 November but it was not until December that they found somewhere to anchor safely. The group helped to establish the colony of New Plymouth and significantly expanded the population of settlers in the area.

Those seeking a new life in the colony did so because they saw little chance of a future in England. They viewed the country as ungodly and moving from bad to worse, and they faced severe persecution for their reformist beliefs. In 1586 a group of dissenting Christians was jailed at The Clink prison in Southwark. The congregation from which many of the Pilgrim Fathers came traces its origins back to the fellowship that met nearby in the home of Roger Rippon from 1592. John Greenwood and

Henry Barrowe, local leaders of an independent church in Southwark, were hung from the gibbet in 1593; John Penry, another leader, was executed the following month; Rippon died in prison; and many of the church's followers fled to Holland around 1608.

While some members of that congregation did eventually board the *Mayflower,* others stayed behind, and the separatist tradition in Southwark continued. In 1616 an independent church was formed in the area by Henry Jacob, who had returned from a period in Leiden, Holland. He led the church for eight years before crossing the Atlantic to join the Pilgrims in America. John Lathrop succeeded him as pastor of the church in south London. Between 1689 and 1702, under the ministry of Revd Jonathan Owen, the church was presented with four communion cups which have since been loaned by Crossway to the Victoria and Albert Museum.[23]

---

[23] Beaker, 1691-92, lent by Crossway United Reformed Church, Sacred Silver & Stained Glass, Room 83, The Whiteley Galleries, case 6C, Victoria and Albert Museum, London,
http://collections.vam.ac.uk/item/O106530/beaker-unknown/

Benjamin Scott and a brand-new building

In the second half of the 19th century, later members of that congregation found a new home in the New Kent Road, mainly due to the generosity of Benjamin Scott, one-time Chamberlain of London. He was a nonconformist and social reformer who advocated for the abolition of church rates, improved educational provision, and the preservation of public spaces. He argued that a church should be built in memory of the Pilgrim Fathers near the site of their original London fellowships, and contributed £2,000 of his own money to the cause. We are able to understand his drive through his own writings. In *Lays of the Pilgrim Fathers: Compiled in Aid of the Fund for Completing the Memorial Church of the Pilgrim Father, in Southwark* he says:[24]

> *It was felicitously suggested that a memorial building, comprising Lecture-hall, Church, and School-rooms, should be erected, as nearly as circumstances would permit, on the site of the place of meeting of the first separatists of Southwark (the precursors, from 1559 to 1620, of the expatriated Pilgrim Fathers of New England), in the vicinity of the prisons (The Clink and the King's Bench) in which so many of their members were immured, and near to the spot where their pastor, Penry, was, for maintaining their principles, brought to a martyr's grave. (St Thomas-a-Watering, Old Kent Road; about half a mile from the selected site of the Memorial Church).*

The Congregational Union of England and Wales considered the subject of sufficient importance to engage their consideration. At a meeting in the year 1855, a motion was unanimously adopted *'to the prompt and generous sympathy and support of the Christian public'.* Scott managed to gain the support of the United States Ambassador, Abbott Lawrence, whom he described as a warm friend. In the event, £40,000 came from the Transatlantic brethren, £2,000 from Scott, £500 from the London Chapel Building Society, and the remaining £3,000 was raised locally.

---

[24] Benjamin Scott, *Lays of the Pilgrim Fathers* (London: Longman, Green, Longman, and Roberts, 1861; digitised and published online by BiblioLife, 16 August 2009. © 2015 FB &C Ltd.)

Design, Memorial Church of the Pilgrim Fathers

Dr John Waddington was the pastor who took the church into the new Pilgrim Fathers' Memorial Church building in Buckenham Square on the New Kent Road. The structure was destroyed in 1940 and the church met in the nearby church house until that too was destroyed in 1944. Dr Albert David Belden, a Congregationalist minister, accepted the post of Honorary Superintendent in 1948 and remained until his death in January 1965, aged 82.

A new church on Great Dover Street

In time, a new church was constructed on Great Dover Street to replace the lost buildings. The archives relating to this project are not available, but a film of the inaugural service can be viewed on YouTube[25].

---

[25] 'The Pilgrim Fathers Memorial Church', YouTube, published 21 July 2015, *https://youtu.be/G-ps8xm1HK8.*

It shows the opening of the building by His Excellency the American Ambassador to Great Britain, Winthrop W. Aldrich, on 15 October 1956. The opening drew the attention of the Queen of England and President Dwight D. Eisenhower, who wrote from the White House in a letter dated 10 October 1956:

> *Please give my greetings to the members and friends of The Pilgrim Fathers' Memorial Church in London.*
>
> *As co-heirs of a great tradition, this congregation has a secure place in the hearts of all who cherish the spirit of religious liberty. Long ago, when the Mayflower carried early pilgrims from your church to our shore, they helped to establish one of the strongest bonds which unite the peoples of our two Nations.*
>
> *In the free and responsible service of God and neighbour, we shall always find our greatest strength.[26]*

Later, on 13 January 1958, Aldrich wrote to the church leadership:

> *I am grateful to you for presenting to me the golden key with which we opened the church door. I feel that this key, which is symbolic of the devoted effort of so many people which resulted in the construction of your church edifice, should be*

---

[26] Letter from President Dwight D. Eisenhower to the leadership of the Pilgrim Fathers' Memorial Church, 10 October 1956, PC 285.8 P12, Southwark Local Library, London.

enshrined in the church. I am therefore returning it to you as a gift...[27]

The Pilgrim Fathers' Memorial Church and Crossway

Sadly, there is no longer any trace of the commemorative key, and very few of the church's records have survived the bombs and the moves. The next reliable documents are also the Pilgrim Fathers' Memorial Church's last – a set of photocopies of a minutes book in which it is announced that:

Pilgrim had decided at their special meeting on 14th Feb. to dissolve their fellowship and to come under the Crossway Management Committee. Resolutions were passed as follows:-

1. *That this meeting of the Pilgrim Church Southwark, meeting on 14th Febry. 1972, resolves that the church shall be dissolved as from the 29th February 1972.*

2. *It is further resolved that the members of the church shall be commended to the Fellowship of Crossway Central Mission for reception into their membership.*

3. *The Church Meeting requests the London Congregational Union to appoint the Management Committee of Crossway Central Mission to care for the building at present occupied by Pilgrim Church.*

Revd Frank Millan would be leaving the Parish in June and it was hoped that a successor would be appointed who would live in the flat at Pilgrim.[28]

So it was that the Pilgrim Fathers' Memorial Church passed into Crossway's charge. The congregation of the church had previously agreed, at a meeting on 8 August 1971, to become part of The United Reformed Church which was officially formed on 21 June the following

---

[27] Letter from Winthrop W. Aldrich, Ambassador of the United States to the United Kingdom, to the leadership of the Pilgrim Fathers' Memorial Church, 13 January 1958, PC 285.8 P12, Southwark Local Library.

[28] Minutes of the Pilgrim Fathers' Memorial Church, 14 February 1972.

year.[29] At that time, Pilgrim Fathers' Memorial Church had also applied to be part of the Elephant Group local ecumenical partnership (a collaborative effort that is explored in Chapter 5). The decision to disband the fellowship was partly a financial necessity as the church accounts were looking precarious. On 21 September 1972 it was reported that the cash in hand stood at £364.23 and cleaning of the church had to be done. It was agreed *to set aside a sum of £1 a week up to a total of £26 to be paid out for this'.[30]* It would appear that there was a 'Mayflower Room' in the Pilgrim Fathers' Memorial Church building: the second Crossway building had its own 'Mayflower Room' which acted as a meeting and utility space. Some of the surviving archives, including the letters from H.M. Queen Elizabeth II and General Eisenhower to commemorate the opening of the New Kent Road building, were lodged with Southwark libraries.[31]

Using the building

On 2 May 1975 or 1976 (the date is not clear) it was reported that a public meeting would be arranged for 12 May *'when suggestions would be considered for [the Pilgrim building's] future use'.[32]* The discussion was prompted by the opening of the new Crossway building on the Heygate Estate, and the church's uncertainty about continued ecumenical relationships. In the event, the building was converted into two residential properties and one commercial property, with the charity Al Anon leasing the main downstairs area for a considerable period between 1975 and 2012.

In 1988 Patricia Belcher, the Crossway treasurer, attempted to open a museum at the church for the display of artefacts and data concerning *'the martyrs of religious freedom, the Pilgrim Fathers and the Mayflower, and the way in which the Congregational Church in Southwark fared from its birth in 1592'.[33]* In this open letter sent to a number of American societies of Mayflower descendants she writes:

---

[29] Church minutes, 1971-72, Crossway United Reformed Church archives.
[30] *Ibid.*
[31] Southwark Local Library was unable to locate the letter from Queen Elizabeth II.
[32] Church minutes, Crossway United Reformed Church archives.
[33] Letter from Patricia A. Belcher, treasurer, Crossway U.R.C. and coordinator, Pilgrim Fathers' Museum, 10 August 1988.

Exciting things are happening in Southwark these days; with the closure of the Docks, tourism must become a major industry in the borough. Accordingly, Southwark Heritage Association has been formed to liaise between the projects under way. These include established ones like the Imperial War Museum and the London Dungeon, to new ventures like the Globe Theatre. The vision to re-open Pilgrim Fathers' Museum is therefore timely because we are but a small cog in an enormous wheel. There is presently a plan afoot to reconstruct the Clink Prison on the actual site, and it is intended that one cell will feature the 'Gathered Church' at worship.[34]

The letter goes on to ask how interested visitors from America would be and what sort of souvenirs would be most attractive. Replies came from North Carolina, Plymouth and West Hyannisport, Massachusetts; Maryland, Oregon, and Sacramento, all of which were very supportive. But there is no evidence to suggest that the idea went any further.

Following Revd Stevenson's appointment in 2009, a major re-development of the residential accommodation at Great Dover Street took place, creating one four-bed and one two-bed apartment, and in 2014 the travel company Baxter Hoare renovated the commercial element of the building and moved their operation there from offices in the Borough Market.[35] Income from the property enables Crossway to fund the work and mission on the United Reformed Church in Elephant and Castle. It is hoped that this book will go some way to consolidating the links between the Pilgrim Fathers, the nonconformist history of Southwark and the ongoing work of Crossway church.

---

[34] *Ibid.*
[35] For further information see their website, *https://www.baxterhoare.com.*

CHAPTER THREE

The Elephant and Castle

The origins of the Elephant

SEVERAL EXPLANATIONS HAVE BEEN GIVEN FOR WHY THE
Elephant and Castle is so called. One of the more romantic ones is that
the name is a corruption of 'La Infanta de Castilla' – supposedly in
reference to a Spanish princess, though exactly which one and what their
connection might be to the area is not clear.

In truth it most likely derives from a blacksmith's workshop. In the
17th century, like today, the Elephant and Castle was a major traffic
junction where the Walworth Road, Kennington Park Road and
Lambeth Road met before leading on to London Bridge, which was then
the only crossing over the River Thames downstream of Kingston. By the
time travellers reached this point, some must have come a long way,
perhaps from as far as the Sussex coast. In 1641 John Flaxman, a
blacksmith, set up a forge to shoe horses on an island between the roads.
The smithy's sign was an elephant with a 'houdah' (a canopied seat) on
its back which could have been misconstrued as a castle. The smithy
eventually developed into an inn so that both horse and rider could be
served before journeying on into the city. The first reference to the name
'Elephant and Castle' is found in the Court Leet Book of the Manor of
Walworth:[36] *'On March 21st 1765, the court met at the Elephant and
Castle, Newington.'*

In the great days of coaching, the Elephant and Castle area became
more and more busy. In the 18th and 19th centuries new bridges were
built over the Thames at Westminster, Blackfriars, Vauxhall and
Waterloo. Roads leading to all of them radiated from the Elephant and
Castle. It became a transport hub with regular traffic jams and a pick-up

---

[36]   Held at the Local Library section at the John Harvard Library, Southwark,
London.

point for many passengers – a place of easy pick-pocketing, skulduggery and depravity.

Over time more roads were built including the New Kent Road linking the (Old) Kent and Walworth roads. Today the Elephant and Castle is not only a road junction but the site of numerous bus stops, an underground station and an overground rail station. In 1875 one of the first routes for the new 24-seater, two-horse double-decker bus was the No. 12 from Peckham to Oxford Circus, which passed through the Elephant and Castle. It continues to operate in 2018. The railway arrived on 6 October 1862 served by the London, Chatham and Dover Railway. The line via Herne Hill, Camberwell and Walworth to Blackfriars and Holborn was built high up on arches above the streets. In 2018 these arches have been converted into businesses, with many in the Elephant and Castle area inhabited by South American traders. The tube arrived on 4 November 1890. Originally called the City and South London Railway, it ran between Stockwell and King William Street before being extended to become the Northern line (the longest continuous tunnel on the network). The Baker Street and Waterloo Railway (now the Bakerloo line) was extended to Elephant and Castle on 5 August 1906.

Life in the Elephant and Castle was not easy. Local living quarters, like the roads themselves, were congested. In 1801, the year of the first census of England, Scotland and Wales, there were 14,847 people living in the Parish of St Mary's Newington. By 1881 the population had reached 107,850; nearly a 650 per cent increase. In 1901 it had reached 122,172, a record number and nearly three times that recorded a century later in 2001. The maps of the time show an area covered with a maze of narrow streets with almost no open space. Large areas were developed to accommodate the growing population, including the area around today's Pasley Park in the neighbourhood of Walworth, which once held one of the area's more unusual attractions. Zoe Lyons has produced a website looking into places of interest throughout the London Borough of Southwark and writes:

> In 1831, Edward Cross had opened the Royal Surrey Zoological Gardens, one of London's first public zoos. At its centre was a large glass conservatory which housed the large carnivores. As well as lions and tigers, the zoo included rhinoceros, pygmy elephants, apes, bears, baboons, monkeys and the first publicly shown giraffes in Britain. Other

attractions included fairs, flower shows, balloon flights, firework displays and re-enactments of historical events. The site was sold in 1878 to local builders Frederick Sutton and John Dudley who laid out new streets and built the Surrey Gardens Estate.[37]

An account by one local resident, A.S. Hall, gives us a glimpse into life in the Elephant and Castle at the turn of the 20th century:

In Newington Butts in 1900 lived the Hall family in one room of a large house, mother, father and three children. It was all that could be afforded on the father's wage as a horse-bus conductor. In this one room they slept, cooked by fire, cleaned from water collected from a cold tap on the landing.[38]

Some of the area's Victorian backstreets and courtyards were little more than slums, where many people lived in small four-room houses, two-up two-down, with a scullery or wash house extension at the back and a shared outside toilet. It is against this background that *The Bitter Cry of Outcast London: An Inquiry into the Condition of the Abject Poor* was written by Revd Andrew Mearns and William C. Preston in 1883. They paint a far more dismal picture of living standards in the area than A.S. Hall's more matter-of-fact account. Part of it is reproduced at length below:

We do not say the condition of their homes, for how can those places be called homes, compared with which the lair of a wild beast would be a comfortable and healthy spot? Few who will read these pages have any conception of what these pestilential human rookeries are, where tens of thousands are crowded together amidst horrors which call to mind what we have heard of the middle passage of the slave ship. To get into them you have to penetrate courts reeking with poisonous and malodorous gases arising from accumulations of sewage and refuse scattered in all directions and often flowing beneath

---

[37] Zoe Lyons, 'Pasley Park', Exploring Southwark, accessed 15 February 2017, *http://www.exploringsouthwark.co.uk/pasley-park/4591065868.*

[38] 'Home at the Beginning of the Century', unpublished memoirs, Local History Library and Archive, John Harvard Library, Southwark, London. Quoted in Mary Boast, *The Story of Walworth* (London: The London Borough of Southwark, 1993).

your feet; courts, many of them which the sun never penetrates, which are never visited by a breath of fresh air, and which rarely know the virtues of a drop of cleansing water. You have to ascend rotten staircases, which threaten to give way beneath every step, and which, in some places, have already broken down, leaving gaps that imperil the limbs and lives of the unwary. You have to grope your way along dark and filthy passages swarming with vermin.

Then, if you are not driven back by the intolerable stench, you may gain admittance to the dens in which these thousands of beings who belong, as much as you, to the race for whom Christ died, herd together. Have you pitied the poor creatures who sleep under railway arches, in carts or casks, or under any shelter which they can find in the open air? You will see that they are to be envied in comparison with those whose lot it is to seek refuge here. Eight feet square – that is about the average size of very many of these rooms. Walls and ceiling are black with the accretions of filth which have gathered upon them through long years of neglect. It is exuding through cracks in the boards overhead; it is running down the walls; it is everywhere. What goes by the name of a window is half of it stuffed with rags or covered by boards to keep out wind and rain; the rest is so begrimed and obscured that scarcely can light enter or anything be seen outside. Should you have ascended to the attic, where at least some approach to fresh air might be expected to enter from open or broken window, you look out upon the roofs and ledges of lower tenements, and discover that the sickly air which finds its way into the room has to pass over the putrefying carcases of dead cats or birds, or viler abominations still.

The buildings are in such miserable repair as to suggest the thought that if the wind could only reach them they would soon be toppling about the heads of their occupants. As to furniture – you may perchance discover a broken chair, the tottering relics of an old bedstead, or the mere fragment of a table; but more commonly you will find rude substitutes for these things in the shape of rough boards resting upon bricks, an old hamper or box turned upside down, or more frequently still, nothing but rubbish and rags.

The authors go on to draw a connection between the area's poverty and its notoriously high crime levels at the time:

Every room in these rotten and reeking tenements houses a family, often two. In one cellar a sanitary inspector reports finding a father, mother, three children, and four pigs! In another room a missionary found a man ill with small-pox, his wife just recovering from her eighth confinement, and the children running about half naked and covered with dirt. Here are seven people living in one underground kitchen, and a little dead child lying in the same room. Elsewhere is a poor widow, her three children, and a child who had been dead thirteen days. Her husband, who was a cabman, had shortly before committed suicide. Here lives a widow and her six children, including one daughter of 29, another of 21, and a son of 27. Another apartment contains father, mother, and six children, two of whom are ill with scarlet fever. In another nine brothers and sisters, from 29 years of age downwards, live, eat and sleep together. Here is a mother who turns her children into the street in the early evening because she lets her room for immoral purposes until long after midnight, when the poor little wretches creep back again if they have not found some miserable shelter elsewhere. Where there are beds they are simply heaps of dirty rags, shavings or straw, but for the most part these miserable beings find rest only upon the filthy boards. The tenant of this room is a widow, who herself occupies the only bed, and lets the floor to a married couple for 2s. 6d. per week. In many cases matters are made worse by the unhealthy occupations followed by those who dwell in these habitations. Here you are choked as you enter by the air laden with particles of the superfluous fur pulled from the skins of rabbits, rats, dogs and other animals in their preparation for the furrier. Here the smell of paste and of drying match-boxes, mingling with other sickly odours, overpowers you; or it may be the fragrance of stale fish or vegetables, not sold on the previous day, and kept in the room overnight. Even when it is possible to do so the people seldom open their windows, but if they did it is questionable whether much would be gained, for the external air is scarcely less heavily charged with poison than the atmosphere within.

Wretched as these rooms are they are beyond the means of many who wander about all day, picking up a living as they can, and then take refuge at night in one of the common lodging houses that abound. These are often the resorts of thieves and vagabonds of the lowest type, and some are kept by receivers of stolen goods. In the kitchen men and women may be seen cooking their food, washing their clothes, or lolling about smoking and gambling. In the sleeping room are long rows of beds on each side, sometimes 60 or 80 in one room. In many cases both sexes are allowed to herd together without any attempt to preserve the commonest decency.

But there is a lower depth still. Hundreds cannot even scrape together the two pence required to secure them the privilege of resting in those sweltering common sleeping rooms, and so they huddle together upon the stairs and landings, where it is no uncommon thing to find six or eight in the early morning.

That people condemned to exist under such conditions take to drink and fall into sin is surely a matter for little surprise. We may rather say, as does one recent and reliable explorer, that they are "entitled to credit for not being twenty times more depraved than they are." One of the saddest results of this overcrowding is the inevitable association of honest people with criminals. Often is the family of an honest working man compelled to take refuge in a thieves' kitchen; in the houses where they live their rooms are frequently side by side, and continual contact with the very worst of those who have come out of our gaols is a matter of necessity.

There can be no question that numbers of habitual criminals would never have become such, had they not by force of circumstances been packed together in these slums with those who were hardened in crime. Who can wonder that every evil flourishes in such hotbeds of vice and disease? Who can wonder that little children taken from these hovels to the hospital cry, when they are well, through dread of being sent back to their former misery? Who can wonder that young girls wander off into a life of immorality, which promises release from such conditions? Who can wonder that the public-house is 'the Elysian field of the tired toiler?'[39]

It was against this background that the first Crossway Central Mission Church was established, led by Superintendent Revd Herbert Kenward, the first man to minister the church and serve the community from its building.

The war years

While Crossway continues to serve the Elephant and Castle community to this day, the place has changed significantly. The 20th century brought with it two world wars. Like many other places, Elephant and Castle was hit hard by the consequent loss of life and of local buildings. The Elephant and Castle Partnership is a current organisation that has brought together a number of public and private organisations to maximise the regeneration potential. On their website they reflect on the impact of the war years:

During the First World War the Elephant and Castle's local brigade, the 24th Battalion of the London Regiment, was based at what is now Braganza Street, off Kennington Park Road. Of the 1,200 men who left for the front in April 1915, only 17 were still serving with the battalion when it returned home in May 1919.

For every man and woman at the front, there was a family left behind. The sheer scale of sacrifice made by some can be hard for us to grasp today. Mrs Heard, of Carter Street, was a mother to 17 children and, according to the South London Press *at the time, had six sons plus two sons-in-law on active service. Five of them were wounded. Another local family, the Patersons, had 11 members on active service as early as 1916.*

---

[39] Revd Andrew Mearns and William C. Preston, *The Bitter Cry of Outcast London: An Inquiry into the Condition of the Abject Poor,* (London: James Clarke & Co., 1883), accessed 29 December 2017, *http://www.attackingthedevil.co.uk/related/outcast.php.*

As the war progressed, streets all around the Elephant developed impromptu shrines to the fallen.

Food price rises during the conflict hit poorer areas such as the Elephant particularly hard, as the advent of submarine warfare cut off food supplies from abroad. Rationing began in February 1917, on a voluntary basis to start with. Both central and local government asked people to do more with less, and the Metropolitan Borough of Southwark held cooking demonstrations to show people how to make the most of their meagre rations.

Perhaps the most frightening new development on the home front was the advent of air raids. The Germans bombed London with both Gotha bombers and Zeppelins. Out of 29 bombing raids on London, 12 involved Southwark. A daylight raid on 13 June 1917 killed six and injured 12, and a Zeppelin raid in October brought the total dead to 24.[40]

Surprisingly, the membership of the church during the First World War actually increased by nearly five per cent, from 348 in 1914 to 363 in 1918, despite the loss of life.

The local casualties were not as great in the next world war, but its impact on the Crossway membership was huge. A comparison of the membership figure for 1939-45 shows a dramatic reduction from 168 to just 56.

Although the church building avoided a direct hit during the Blitz, a nearby 'delay-action' bomb in Gurney Street destroyed much of the surrounding area.

During the worst blitzkrieg raid on London, on 10/11 May 1941, bombers struck at the railway line that ran north from Elephant and Castle and as a result a fierce firestorm destroyed many of the buildings. Unsurprising then that after the war the area was a shadow of its former glory as a place for shopping and entertainment.

---

[40] 'WWI and the Elephant', Elephant and Castle Partnership, first published in *The Elephant Magazine*, Summer 2014, accessed 16 February 2018, *https://www.elephantandcastle.org.uk/a-brief-history/ww1-and-the-elephant/.*

The cross marks Crossway which just misses the worst of the damage.

The post-war Elephant

Rebuilding took some time, and the community lived among the dust and grime of the demolished and battered area for many decades. And even as new buildings began to rise, the area's economic difficulties persisted. In September 1961 Revd Boorman described the changing nature of the area in a *Crossway Chronicle* article. He reflects:

> *We are very conscious of our situation here and quite certain that the work of this Mission will be increasingly needed in this rapidly changing area. It will not be very long now before the Elephant and Castle will have a facade of prosperity and modern elegance. It may be that folk passing through will judge the area by that facade. Undoubtedly large sections of our Borough of Southwark are changing for the better and that percentage of the population that are being rehoused by the L.C.C. have better accommodation than has been available for generations; but behind the facade or alongside the rehousing there are still dirty street[s], filthy tenements and*

lonely lost people. Old people who need some encouraging interest from someone; children who need guidance in a world of decayed and still decaying standards and folk who cannot find a niche in the 'never-had-it-so-good' state.[41]

Two articles in the *Crossway Chronicle,* written by Boorman's successor, Revd Ashdown, offer further insights into the state of the neighbourhood. In September 1964 he wrote:

As we look back on the days when the work here first began, we thank for God for real progress in the conditions of the people who live around the Elephant. Yet there is no room for complacency. There is still dreadful overcrowding and lots of bad housing. I have been shocked at some places in which people have to live – worse than anything I experienced in East London. The lack of open spaces and playgrounds, the pockets of need and poverty, the loneliness – especially of old people, all present us with a need which is an opportunity. The seeming irrelevance of the church in the lives of most of our neighbours is a continual challenge.[42]

Twelve months later he addressed the topic again:

Nobody can live where we do without becoming involved in the problems of our community life. Bad housing, immigration, delinquency, drink and drugs. The presence of several local hostels and lodging houses brings us into contact with many vagrants and needy people with their problems. The very name MISSION over our door brings a number of visitors seeking all kinds of help. During the year we persevered with some of these and held them in your name. Some we are glad to say with some success.[43]

Over the following decades, the area continued to develop unevenly as an overcrowded area home to large and diverse communities.

---

[41] *Crossway Chronicle,* September 1961, held at Crossway United Reformed Church archives.

[42] *Ibid.,* September 1964.

[43] *Ibid.,* September 1965.

The modern Elephant

Multiculturalism is a defining feature of the area. In 2018 the author would say that the world now meets at the Elephant. The Elephant and Castle is home to a huge variety of cultural, ethnic and religious groups. Among them is the South American community drawn from Colombia, Ecuador, Bolivia, Puerto Rico and Portuguese-speaking Brazil. There is also an African community mainly drawn from western countries such as Nigeria and Ghana, but also including people from the east (Uganda, Ethiopia and Eritrea) and south (Zimbabwe and Zambia). An older immigrant community from the West Indies has largely moved on, while the widening of the European Union has brought people from eastern and middle Europe to the area. Most recently, the Elephant has seen a growing number of immigrants from Japan, China and Korea. White British residents are now the largest minority group. The effect of such rapid change has resulted in a collection of disparate communities rather than one community.

At the time of writing, more than £3bn is being spent on the regeneration of the Elephant and Castle. This investment is generating new homes, better transport links, improved shopping and leisure facilities, new schools and community centres, and thousands of new jobs and training opportunities. By 2025 more than 5,000 new and replacement homes will have been built in the neighbourhood. The Elephant will be home to the largest new park created in central London in 70 years, as well as three new public squares, new pocket parks and green spaces. However, walking down the Walworth Road to the manse, it does not always feel like the area has been gentrified. A wine bar and a couple of coffee shops have sprung up among the betting offices, payday lenders, nail bars and chicken shops, but crime levels are still high and it is still too common to find a family of four in a one-bedroom flat.[44] Within the Crossway congregation only the minister has a private garden and only two members own a car. Few of the members go on holiday and the average weekly contribution 'in-the-plate' is just £3.

While the developers and urban planners may design prosperity into the neighbourhood, only time will tell whether the hopes and dreams will

---

[44] There were 398 crimes in December 2017 within half a mile of the centre of Crossway URC according to Streetcheck, accessed 16 February 2018, *https://www.streetcheck.co.uk/crime/se16sb.*

become reality. Can an area with poverty and deprivation in its DNA change into a 'go-to' location?

CHAPTER FOUR

The Ministers

IN MANY CHURCHES THERE IS A ROGUES' GALLERY IN WHICH the images of former ministers adorn the vestry wall, peering down on the new incumbent, daring them to change the church or tackle the issues that were insoluble in the past. Some of them appear to have sat for their portraits a little too late, as if they were captured in the funeral home just before their final journey. No such archive exists for the clergy of Crossway. In an attempt to correct this deficiency, this chapter will outline and capture the flavour and personality of the reverend past.

Crossway started life as Murphy's Memorial Chapel. Available records suggest that it was established in 1720 in Gurncy Street, with a seating capacity of 500.[45] Where information is known, the names of ministers are recorded alongside the date at which they arrived:

Date	Minister
1870	David Bayne Morris
1890	J.H. Wilson D.D.
1895	W. Mottram
1900	G. Fuller

Little is known about these four ministers, but the church's next leader is well remembered. In the early years of the 20th century, the chapel was redeveloped and the seating capacity reduced to 200. It became the Crossway Central Mission Church, under the ministry of the longstanding Herbert H. Kenward.

---

[45] Congregational Union handbook, 1906, Dr Williams's Library, London.

Herbert H. Kenward: 1905-1925

Revd Kenward was born 8 June 1874 and was trained for ministry at Paton Congregational College, Nottingham, taking up his first post at Magdalen Road in Norwich. In an unsigned article (author and date unknown, but likely to be after 1972) we learn that:

> Bert, as he was affectionately known by all and sundry, came from a strong nonconformist background. His father Amram Kenward had been a pillar of the Lewes Tabernacle, at that time a very flourishing church.
>
> For many generations the Kenwards of Lewes had been market gardeners who also had a retail shop selling their produce as well as serving shops and markets in the Brighton area.[46]

Bert had three brothers: Jack, the eldest, who took over the family business; Walter, a successful watchmaker and jeweller; and Frank, who became the county beekeeper. In 1903 Bert married Florence Letheren from his home town of Lewes. When he took up the post at Murphy's Memorial Chapel, the couple moved into 7 Angel Park Gardens, Brixton – three miles from the church by horse-drawn tram. Revd Kenward named the new church Crossway because the original buildings were on a crossroads. The article goes on:

> When the new block was built it contained quarters for the 'sisters', about four ladies who wore a brown habit [and] who visited the backstreets of the neighbourhood. It was necessary for them to dress in this way to make them different from other folk, as in that part of London many thieves and robbers dwelt, and they would have been attacked had they not worn such a habit.

In addition to the records of his tasks at Crossway, Revd Kenward appears in the minutes of Southwark Park Congregational Church, where he also gave his time:

> Early in 1915 the Revd Herbert Kenward of Crossway took over the management of Southwark Park presiding at

---

[46] From family documents supplied by Mrs Ann Sawyer, the granddaughter of Revd Kenward.

> *Deacon's and Church meetings and also arranging pulpit
> supplies. Mr Kenward was looked upon as our Superintendent
> Minister and this arrangement lasted until he left Crossway.
> Unfortunately not one of his successors at Crossway has been
> able to follow his example.*[47]

Revd Kenward's ministry was an eventful one, taking the church through the whole of the First World War. One incident in particular from this period stands out. In 1917 the conflict had swung in favour of the Germans. For the first time, air warfare played a major role and zeppelin raids had taken place over London. A large printworks close to Crossway received a direct hit during one of these raids, and many lives were lost. To boost morale, Revd Kenward had the idea of broadcasting his services into the main road using relatively new 'wireless' technology. A microphone was installed in the pulpit for the purpose, and a loudspeaker in the porch at the entrance to the church building. One evening a man walked into the service when it was halfway through, and after it had finished he asked one of the sidesmen if he could have a chat with the minister. He was shown into the vestry, at which point he withdrew a revolver from his pocket and placed it on the table. He explained that he had intended to take one last walk along the New Kent Road before going home to shoot his wife, child and himself, but the music had drawn him into the church. After the service he felt he had a future after all, and intended to start a new life.

In another article supplied by his granddaughter, two additional memorable incidents from Revd Kenward's ministry are described. The first was a fearful venture into the shady world of the Elephant in 1910, when Mr Ernest Jeffs offered to show Revd Kenward the darker side of life in the neighbourhood. He told Revd Kenward to grow some stubble, put on some old and shabby clothing, and wear a choker around his neck. Disguised in this manner, the two of them took to the streets and entered a pub so that they could observe a rogue up close. Naturally they had to buy drinks so as not to blow their cover, but Revd Kenward was teetotal and so he attempted to spill the contents of his glass onto the sawdust-covered floor. Suddenly Mr Jeffs called out to 'run for it': he had noticed that one of the local characters had smashed a glass against the side of

---

[47] Minutes of the Southwark Park Congregational Church, Howes and Herring S.C. P285.8 SOV, Local History Library and Archive, John Harvard Library, Southwark, London.

the bar and was about to attack them with it. They managed to get to the door first and make their escape, but it was an experience never to be repeated.

The second incident occurred towards the end of Revd Kenward's ministry, around 1920. It involved the persistent loss of money from ladies' coats and handbags left in the church building. In a clandestine operation the Church Secretary witnessed a church member, Mrs Baker, take a purse and hide it in her clothing. The coins had been marked so that they could be easily identified, so when Mrs Baker spent the ill-gotten gains in a local shop, the case against her was watertight. Or so they thought. The police were called and she was charged with the offence. But Mrs Baker employed a good lawyer, and in the court hearing he was able to confuse the witness into denying three times seeing the prisoner taking the money. The judge had no option but to find Mrs Baker not guilty. The article explains the troubling impact that the event had on the church's minister:

> *This case had a bad effect on Mr Kenward; almost overnight his hair turned from black to grey and his health suffered accordingly.[48] Having served the institute for 21 years he felt that the time had come for him to leave. He was invited to the ministry at Cricklewood Congregational Church. However, the work [ministry] at Crossway continued under the Revd Roff for some years, but the need for the Institute and welfare work had been largely taken over by the State, the neighbourhood had also changed, many of the old buildings had been torn down and replaced by council flats, the property was too large to maintain so the council bought the site and the whole of the building was demolished and rather ugly flats have taken its place. The spiritual side of the work however still continues in a smaller building not far from the old Church.*

In addition to these second-hand accounts, we are also able to learn about Revd Kenward's ministry in his own words, thanks to some notes kindly supplied by his granddaughter. In a statement that was presumably delivered to an audience that had asked him to tell them about his work, he explained:

---

[48] A photocopy of an entry from a family account indicates that he suffered a heart attack.

I should like for a short while this evening to take you back to the year 1905, and to a part of London which is known as the Elephant and Castle. In the 1900s this was a poverty stricken area where living conditions were simply appalling, whole families living in one room. Sanitary conditions were almost unknown, crime and criminals were on the upgrade, and woe betide a policeman who walked alone in the side street. The only uniform that was respected was that worn by the Salvation Army.

Drink appeared to be the population's only solace and to many public houses that abound [in] that neighbourhood men, women and even children repaired each night; for remember that the licensing laws in those far off days were not as they are today. The pubs were open all day and nearly all night.

Unemployment also was a very terrible thing. Lloyd George had not brought in his bill to insure the unemployed person a little when he was out of work, no 5/[49] per week family allowance, only the 'Board of Guardians' and charity. Perhaps it was not surprising that the church had not the appeal that it should have had to these people for the churches were mainly empty, and it is about one of these that I wish to talk for a while tonight.

It was known as the 'Murphy's Memorial Hall', situated about a quarter of a mile from the Elephant. Some good folks had been trying for a few years to bring a little light into the people's lives, but in a religious census taken in 1902/03 it gave the number of men and women attending this place as 45 in the morning and 170 at evening service, while the seating capacity of the Hall was 900.[50] After two more years the members of the church felt that it was hopeless to carry on; in addition to dwindling congregations they were heavily burdened by debt and as a last resort they appealed to the

---

[49] Author's note: five shillings converts to 25p.
[50] This number differs from the estimate given in the Congregational Union handbook of 1906. It is not clear which figure is accurate or whether the church was extended.

London Congregational Union to take over the building and the debt.

This was no light matter: the Union had already started two such Missions, one at Claremont off Kings Cross and the other at Whitfields, Tottenham Court Road – whose superintendent incidentally was the Rev. Sylvester Horne, a Liberal Member of Parliament and, a matter of interest to this generation, the Father of Kenneth Horne of Much Binding in the Marsh.

They felt however that in spite of all other commitments, here was a real call and one that they must not miss on any account. So they agreed to take over the building and the debt and have the place done up and made suitable for Central Mission work.

Having the building seen to, the next thing was to find a suitable man to take over the work. They found the man at Norwich, a man in his thirties who had already built a new church out of a 'tin tabernacle' and whose work was extending widely in that city. He had no desire to leave this, his first church and the people whom he loved but felt that in S.E. London was a job of work that should be done, and that with God's help he could do it.

He commenced his ministry in November 1905. Within ten months he had an institute open and a year later a creche where the poor mothers could leave babies from 6:30 a.m. to 6 p.m. each day. The babies were well cared for by a trained staff: their old clothing [was] taken off as soon as they arrived, [and they were] bathed and given breakfast and looked after until their mothers called for them later. Also a clinic was opened one day each week where the babies were weighed, given food and in some cases clothing.

In 1911 at the Annual meeting, Mr Kenward reported that this had been the best and busiest year so far. The children's and young people's departments showed a weekly attendance of 2700 and the various departments that saw to the wants of the adults 7000. The Sisters had made 11000 visits in the year. The total membership (on confession of faith) [was] 373. The women's meeting average weekly attendance [was] over 500. [In the case of] Saturday evening entertainment for children the number was 1050. Mission and institute – every side of man's wants were catered for, religion, sport and a 'poor man's lawyer'. Financial help came from far and wide to carry on this great work. One of the largest benefactors was Mr W.J. Brown of Woodford who practically built the large institute himself.

In 1916 a house was given to Mr Kenward at South Godstone by a man who had admired the work that he had done at Crossway. Mr Kenward pass[ed] this gift over to Crossway for use as a holiday home where people from the grime and dust of South London could get a cheap week's holiday in the beautiful Surrey Hills...

1920/25

About this time, a great change came over this part of London. Education was beginning to be felt, the licensing laws had been tightened up and the amount of drunkenness had almost ceased to be a problem. Factories had opened at Dagenham and the Great West Road so that the population tended to decrease. The work, however, still goes on; perhaps in not such a big way as before but the need is still there.[51]

The timing of this presentation by Revd Kenward is not known, nor is its aim or purpose. But Revd Kenward clearly wants the audience to know of this part of his ministry. Perhaps he gave it to help raise funds for the ongoing work on the church building. It is interesting that he makes no reference to the First World War, nor of a visit to the church by Queen Mary which took place during his ministry (this event is explored in another section of this book). It would appear that it is written at the end of his Crossway ministry, before he went on to Cricklewood until 1930. Later in his career, he took on roles within various unions to promote Church Extension (the modern-day equivalent is probably a Mission Enabler). He became Secretary of the Sussex

---

[51] An undated article written by Revd Kenward and provided by Mrs Sawyer from the family's archive.

Congregational Union in 1939, serving until his retirement in 1946. He died on 24 May 1954 in Seaford, Sussex.

Research for this also book revealed an archive record of Revd Kenward joining Major General Sir W. Thwaites and the Lord Bishop of Kingston for the unveiling in Kennington Park of a memorial to the fallen of the 24th London Regiment (also known as The Queen's Regiment). The event took place at 4:00 p.m. on Saturday 19 July 1924.[52]

During the ministry of Revd Kenward the church membership grew significantly. The exact numbers as recorded in the Congregational Yearbooks of the time[53] are shown overleaf. He was assisted by several people whose roles are also recorded in archive documents.

Edward Hamson: 1907-1911

Born in Hinckley, Leicestershire, in 1874, this was Hamson's first ministry. He went on to serve in Stepney, South Elmsall and Queen Street, Sheffield, before moving to Cavendish Street in Manchester. His last post was Whitby Road, Ellesmere Port. He died on 11 June 1952.

Thomas King: 1912-1915

King had already served pastorates in Atherstone and Melksham before going to Crossway. He left Elephant and Castle to do war service in the First World War. After the conflict, he went to Mukden Medical College, Manchuria, China, before returning to the UK and serving the churches at Mitcham and Sompting.

Rowland William Young: 1915-1916

Born in Chiddingstone in Kent in 1872, Young served churches in Suffolk and Durham before returning south. Prior to Crossway he was minister at South Norwood and after leaving he was minister in

---

[52] 'Kennington Park London re-dedication of 24th London memorial' discussion, 2 July 2014, Great War London forum. Accessed 13 April 2018, *http://1914-1918.invisionzone.com/forums/topic/213817-kennington-park-london-re-dedication-of-24th-london-memorial/*.

[53] London Congregational Union yearbooks, 1905-1923, Dr Williams's Library, London. Where dates are missing the figures were either unrecorded or unchanged.

Hammersmith, Sandwich, Maidstone, and Denham, before finally working as a chaplain in Lenham Hospital.

Year	Membership	Children in Sunday School	Sunday School Leaders	Lay Preachers
1905	160	297	25	0
1906	110	324	24	0
1907	150	310	17	2
1909	170	350	22	2
1910	195	380	24	2
1911	244	450	27	2
1912	262	380	42	0
1913	310	517	43	2
1914	348	618	65	3
1915	360	692	64	3
1916	359	627	59	4
1917	380	683	37	10
1918	363	574	33	4
1919	383	600	52	8
1920	350	600	45	6
1921	345	830	48	8
1922	353	850	50	6
1923	294	962	48	0

Church membership statistics (1905-1923).

Samuel James Cowdy: 1917-1919

Born 15 October 1873, in Kennington, Cowdy went straight into the mission field after finishing his studies at Cheshunt College and served for six years between 1901 and 1907 in the Telugu district of India with the London Missionary Society (LMS). He returned to Winchcombe in Gloucestershire before moving to Park Chapel, Crouch End, as an assistant. He subsequently moved to Lewes and spent a short time in France with Young Men's Christian Association before moving to Crossway. After Crossway he became Middlesex District Secretary of the LMS for 20 years, finishing his ministry in Guildford in 1942. He died on 8 February 1954.

William Riddell Hunter: 1918-1919

Born in Glasgow, Hunter spent his career in Bradford, Hampshire, Lanarkshire and Surrey, crisscrossing Hadrian's Wall. Crossway was his last post and he died 20 November 1919 aged 49.

There are no surviving minute books or records that help to tell the story of the ministers that served the church between 1925 and 1957. Instead, we have to rely on *The Surman Index Online* for a thumbnail sketch of this period. What information that can be found is gathered below.[54]

Tom Walter Roff: 1925-1938

Born in Manchester on 10 October 1883, Roff trained at Paton Congregational College, Nottingham. He started his ministry at Beeston Hill, Leeds, moving to Salford Central Mission before coming to Crossway. He went on to Mawdsley Street, Bolton, and later to Stoke, Deal, and Telscombe Cliffs. He was twice married and died on 6 August 1959.

John Potts: 1938-1942

Born in Nottingham in 1888, Revd Potts studied at Paton Congregational College and served four different pastorates in

---

[54] The Surman Index Online, accessed 13 February 2018, *http://www.qmulreligionandliterature.co.uk/research/surman-index-online/*.

Lancashire between 1915 and 1938: Dalton-in-Furness; Grimshaw Street, Preston; Newton, Lancaster; and Queen's Park, Manchester. After his short service at Crossway he worked for the YMCA; Abbot's Road, Leicester; and Lynton in Devon. He died on 16 January 1960, just eight days after the death of his wife.

Ronald Charles Christopher: 1940-1943

Revd Potts was assisted by Ronald Charles Christopher who straddled two ministers between 1940 and 1943. He was born 27 July 1910 in Bow, east London, and studied at Paton. Crossway was his first pastorate. He went on to serve at Hoddesdon, Hertfordshire, and North Shields, Northumberland, before working for the British and Foreign Bible Society in the UK midlands (1950-1962) and north-west (1962-1965). His last pastorate was at Salford Central Mission. He died on 11 December 1999 in Worthing, West Sussex.

William Benjamin James Martin: 1942-1950

Born in Swansea in 1904, Martin studied at Hackney Theological Academy and New College, London. Starting his ministry in Hounslow, he went to Bethnal Green before joining Crossway. His last pastorate was Augustine-Bristo, Edinburgh, from 1951.

Douglas and Margaret Mabel Watts: 1951-1957

Between 1951 and 1957 the husband and wife team Revds Douglas and Margaret Mabel Watts led Crossway.

The Congregational Union statistics from 1925 to 1956, opposite, show a decline in the church's membership and Sunday School attendance.

Year	Membership	Children in Sunday School	Sunday School Leaders	Lay Preachers
1925	273	975	63	5
1926	240	1006	65	5
1927	247	1010	69	5
1928	226	1009	68	5
1929	210	735	64	3
1930	199	520	53	4
1931	203	655	54	4
1932	177	641	51	0
1933	179	625	45	0
1934	173	544	55	0
1935	173	550	55	0
1936	178	372	39	0
1937	170	372	39	0
1938	173	332	31	2
1939	168	386	36	2
1940	170	300	26	3
1941	100	300	15	2
1943	50	160	8	2
1944	58	160	9	4
1945	56	160	8	2
1947	64	168	12	2
1948	68	171	12	3
1949	71	210	14	3
1951	74	221	15	2
1955	80	250	12	1
1956	75	250	14	1

Church membership statistics (1925-1956).

It is interesting, and unexpected, that the decline of Crossway church did not happen during the First World War but during the Second World War. Between 1914 and 1918 membership surprisingly rose slightly and the decline was seen between 1939 and 1945. While there is no space to explore the statistics themselves in great depth in this book, it is clear that the lower membership numbers preoccupied the minds and challenged the approaches of all successive ministers as they tried to revive the church and meet the requirements of a community that remained one of the poorest in London.

Stanley Boorman: 1957-1963

A minutes book covering church meetings from 3 March 1960 to 20 February 1966, together with copies of the *Crossway Chronicle* from January 1958 to September 1965 and a House Committee Minutes book held at Southwark Local History Library help us to glimpse the ministries of Stanley Boorman and Ernest Ashdown.

Boorman inherited the original Crossway building, but by this point it had become very difficult to maintain. In the fourth edition of *Crossway Chronicle* (January 1958) can be found Revd Boorman's first letter as minister of Crossway. In it he acknowledges the difficulties facing the church, saying:

> *I break no confidences when I tell you that the financial position here is acute and needs constant attention. We have to carry a vast building not of our choice but our fathers' choice, and now very much a burden.*

A year later he bemoaned the building as having endless problems and endless bills, but rejoiced at the formation of a new House Committee. He expressed the hope that *'the committee will more and more be able to release me from such problems so that I may be freer to do more ministerial and less managerial work'.*[55] In a later article under the title 'Our Neighbourhood' he wrote:

> *The Elephant and Castle district is still a very mixed area. Part of it rebuilt by L.C.C. into new flats, part of it still the old tenements some long since condemned... Many [of the people*

---

[55] Revd Stanley Boorman, *Crossway Chronicle,* January 1958, held at Crossway United Reformed Church archives.

living there] entirely pagan but all needy though often not knowing their need... It is a tremendously impossible task at times made gloriously possible by the prayer, thought and giving of friends.[56]

The House Committee minutes from 1961 report a break-in to the minister's manse on 21 April.[57] The intruder stole various monies amounting to £6. Reading the newsletters from this time suggests that Revd Boorman struggled to enjoy his ministry at Crossway. In February 1962 he wrote:

I can't say that the work gets easier, because it has so many ups and downs and when we think we have achieved a victory it is often a prelude to defeat and an imperious demand to rethink the attack.[58]

Many of the ups and downs of this period were recorded in the *Crossway Clarion,* as it was known at the time. The publication had previously been known as the *Crossway Chronicle,* but in 1961 the April issue was edited by Donald Bere, who changed the name and said that for it to be a success it must be sold to all members (at a cost of 6d, or 2.5p). Bere appears not to have worked on the next edition in May 1961 and the publication is reduced to one A4 page. The first edition did not sell out and a loss was made.

There is a lovely vignette in the December 1961 / February 1962 editions of the *Crossway Clarion* asking for help:

We are always glad to receive secondhand clothes, especially for our old folk and are able to help many because of gifts, but one of our Grandfathers' Club we have been able to help very little indeed, because we cannot find any clothes to fit him. He is 5ft 11ins high, 48 inc. chest, 52 ins. waist. If anyone can

[56] Revd Stanley Boorman, 'Our Neighbourhood', *Crossway Chronicle,* January 1958, Crossway United Reformed Church archives.
[57] House Committee minutes book, 1961, John Harvard Library, Southwark, London.
[58] Revd Stanley Boorman, *Crossway Chronicle,* February 1962, Crossway United Reformed Church archives.

help with clothes of such ample proportions, we will gratefully pass them on to "Tiny".[59]

The response was positive, and it was reported that Mr 'Tiny' Paine received almost a complete outfit.

In the spring 1962 edition of the *Clarion* we are told the story of Revd Stanley Boorman himself.[60] He was introduced to the church aged 11 at Hither Green Congregational. He enjoyed his formative years in the youth group under the guidance of Miss Hardy and became a Sunday School teacher. He was an assistant in the Scout Troop and ran for Blackheath Harriers. He was apprenticed to Waygood Otis to become a lift engineer but decided this was not for him and was subsequently accepted into theological college, spending two years of his training in Montreal, Canada. After another three years at New College to complete his studies, he took up his first church at Ingatestone in Essex.

In 1940 he moved to Fulham Palace Road, a month before the Blitz. Not one service was missed although a few of them were interrupted by sirens and heavy gunfire. During this ministry he met and married his wife, Yvonne Doreen Andrews. The couple moved in 1950 to Blackburn in Lancashire where he became minister of Audley Range Congregational Church. In December 1958 he came with his wife and four children to Crossway. The article continues by assessing his work at the church:

He took up a task that was far greater than he ever realised. Tremendous strides have been made in lessening Crossway's financial debt, in putting the building into order, and in ensuring that Crossway's financial future is less worrying than it has been for a long time. By making extensive "lets" from the building, Crossway has made a beginning towards being self-supporting. Will he be able to leave a strong and happy fellowship when his ministry at Crossway ends? We all of us know that this is his most fervent hope and prayer.[61]

In Crossway's House Committee meeting book Revd Boorman is reported to have reflected on the potential teenage membership, adding in a very un-politically correct manner that *'[t]he people of the district*

---

[59] *Crossway Clarion,* December 1961, Crossway United Reformed Church archives.
[60] *Ibid.*
[61] *Ibid.*

including so many Turks and Greeks would no doubt make religious persuasion difficult'.[62]

On 18 October 1963 the minutes of the House Committee reported that Revd Boorman had accepted the call to Balham Congregational Church. The minute reads:

> *In considering the above it was requested that the following be recorded:*
>
> - *Mr Boorman's six years of service 1/12/57 - 1/12/63*
>
> - *Local people consider that Crossway buildings have been completely transformed*
>
> - *Mr Jolly as Streatham Church member also acclaimed the vast changes brought about in the accounts*
>
> - *Mr Boorman's pastoral work including his chaplaincy at Guys*[63]

The Boorman family left Crossway in November 1963 and he finished his ministry in Welling. He died on 31 January 1985.

Ernest Ashdown: 1963-1971

Boorman was replaced at Crossway by Ernest Ashdown, who chaired his first meeting of the House Committee on 14 February 1964 and reported that...

> *...the visitors to Crossway have been the Salvation Army, three separate police visits, a false alarm with the London Fire Brigade and a health visitor was also required to call in connection with a woman found crawling along the New Kent Road. (Welcome to Crossway.)*[64]

He went on to chair his first church meeting on 8 March 1964 and wrote his first newsletter that September. In it, he recognises and gives

---

[62] House Committee Minutes Book, 14 December 1962, A662, Local History Section, John Harvard Library, Southwark, London.

[63] *Ibid.*

[64] Ernest Ashdown, 1964, Crossway United Reformed Church archives.

thanks for the work of Mr and Mrs Boorman, suggesting that their contribution will be *'memorable in the history of this place'.*[65]

A year later in the newsletter, Revd Ashdown reported on his progress and the challenges he had discovered at Crossway:

> *Last year was I suppose, an average one. Each week over 150 youngsters join in our activities and about the same number of elderly folk join in our afternoon meeting or are regularly visited. This is about as many as we can deal with considering our small staff of helpers. Our Sunday Services have continued although we cannot report any increase in numbers.*[66]

Revd Ashdown was the minister responsible for negotiating the demolition of the original Crossway and the building of a new one a little farther down the New Kent Road, although it would be left to his successor Revd Ralph Essex to preside at the opening of the new building. Revd Ashdown gave a detailed outline of the plans to the House Committee on 16 May 1968, stating...

> *...that after a long period of rumours about Crossway involvement in Southwark's 'resettlement' plans a more positive stage had been recently reached. At a meeting called by the Borough of Southwark's planners social workers (including ministers) had been informed of the broad outline of the proposed HEYGATE ESTATE*
>
> *(1) New Kent Road to become a 6-lane road*
>
> *(2) Additional road linking New Kent Road and Walworth Rd to become a 4-lane or 6-lane*
>
> *(3) Proposed population density 136 per acre instead of 500 as at present*
>
> *(4) Alternative accommodation for tenants in housing to start soon*
>
> *(5) Need for churches in the future discussed (Baptists have intimated that they are not seeking resettlement)*

---

[65] Ernest Ashdown, Crossway newsletter, September 1964, Crossway United Reformed Church archives.

[66] *Ibid.,* September 1965.

Mr Nutley stated compulsory purchase order for Heygate Scheme should go to Minister of Housing at the end May 1968 and his decision expected February 1969. It was further anticipated that up to 1971 people would be leaving (I.L.E.A. – Inner London Education Authority – junior school would not move).

Interim Accommodation – *St Matthew's Hall of 3 floors and church could be sufficient for 2 churches*

> *NB1   combined church attendance 47 morning and evening*
>
> *NB2   St Matthew's church heating is low standard*
>
> *NB3   Crossway is in the parish of St Matthew's*

Long term accommodation

> *A. Joint churches building on St Matthew's site*
>
> *B. St Matthew's as now plus dwelling for Congregational minister in Heygate*
>
> > *NB1   Student lay pastor for Pilgrim is to be consulted*
> >
> > *NB2   Early in June vicar of St Matthew's to be visited by Mr Hall*
> >
> > *NB3   Mr Nutley to visit Southwark B.C. for map of CPO for Heygate*

Finance – could be lump sum or accommodation[67]

Brian Pavett: 1970-1971

Revd Ashdown did not remain in-post to see through the development of the new building. His immediate successor Revd Brian Pavett held only short tenure at Crossway, but oversaw a period of change. In April 1971 he recorded that seven people out of a membership of 17 found themselves living too far away from the church to take an

---

[67] Ernest Ashdown, report to the House Committee, 16 May 1968, Crossway United Reformed Church archives.

active part in it after being rehoused.[68] In the same report, he made the sad announcement of the death of the church's oldest member Polly Hatch at 99 years of age, and spoke of the doldrums that Crossway found itself in. By then the congregation had moved in with St Matthew's and regular staff meetings had been set up. Evidently the old Crossway buildings were still not entirely demolished, and neither was the new site prepared.

Writing six months later, Revd Pavett took pleasure in sharing the glad news that Revd Ralph Essex had accepted an invitation to become a full-time member of the ministerial team. He wrote:

> *This a cause for much satisfaction, since the plans for the new Crossway buildings have now been finalised, the redevelopment of the Heygate area which it will serve has begun, and the opportunity is given for a very much fuller co-operation in worship and service during the remaining 18 months or so before the new Crossway buildings are ready, as the foundation of a new pattern of life.*[69]

Ralph Essex: 1971-1978

Revd Essex was inducted to the pastorate on 11 November 1971. He was a great supporter of the partnership between Crossway, St Matthew's Church, the Pilgrim Fathers' Memorial Church and Holy Trinity, and hoped that the group would be formally recognised as an Ecumenical Experiment (his term). In his opening letter as minister he writes that nearly all the old tenement buildings which surround Crossway were demolished and new blocks were rising quickly. The space allocated for Crossway stood empty, but he had been assured that it would be ready by October 1973. By this point the membership was down to six but he remained optimistic and thanked Mr Hedley Smith, the chair of the management committee, for his help and encouragement. Essex's hope was:

---

[68] Brian Pavett, pastoral letter, April 1971, Crossway United Reformed Church archives.

[69] Brian Pavett, pastoral letter, October 1971, Crossway United Reformed Church archives.

> *...the church will play its part in creating a community that
> people will be happy to live in, in a place where at the moment
> there is nothing but empty space and blocks of concrete.*[70]

An interesting entry in the minutes of the church meeting held on 22
November 1972 records the announcement that the Heygate Estate had
been renamed the Locksfield Estate. This name was never officially
adopted, however; perhaps the council had a change of heart. The same
report indicates that by this point people had started to move onto the
estate.[71] But it seems that work on the Crossway building was slower to
begin. It was not until the Crossway management committee meeting on
Monday 14 May 1973 that Mr Nutley, a committee member, confirmed
that an order had been given to start work on the new Crossway site. It
had been given the go-ahead the previous Friday, but there was some
delay owing to difficulty in obtaining steel![72] Throughout this time, when
the congregations of Crossway and other local churches were sharing a
building, work on the Ecumenical Experiment continued. This is
explored in more detail in Chapter 5.

On 7 February 1974, Revd Essex prepared a paper in which he argued
for the need for another URC member of staff. He concluded:

> *In my opinion another theologically trained member of the
> team is desirable because the implications of our experiment
> have to be worked out in so many day to day things that I
> think it is wrong to leave the responsibility of it to one person
> on the U.R.C. side. The contribution of the Management
> Committee is invaluable in major concerns but for practical
> purposes it is the life we live together that counts. I believe it
> is right to ask for the appointment of an associate minister.*[73]

---

[70] Ralph Essex, pastoral letter, April 1972, Crossway United Reformed
Church archives.

[71] Minutes from a Church Meeting, 22 November 1972, Crossway United
Reformed Church archives.

[72] Minutes of a Management Committee meeting, 14 May 1973, Crossway
United Reformed Church archives.

[73] Ralph Essex, 'Justification for additional Crossway staff', 7 February 1974,
Crossway United Reformed Church archives.

Kay Salvage: 1975-1982

There are no further minutes or notes following on from Revd Essex's paper, but it clearly received a positive response. On Saturday 25 January 1975, at 6:00 p.m., a service of ordination of Miss Kay Salvage as deaconess was held in the United Reformed Church. At the same time, she was inducted into the Team Ministry of the Joint Congregation with Holy Trinity and St Matthew's Church of England. The service was presided over by Revd Vernon Lowis, the Moderator of Southern Province URC. The charge was given by The Revd Iain Stewart, Minister of Canterbury URC. A picture of Miss Salvage appears on a copy of *Crossroads,* the joint pastorate magazine. The accompanying article tells us more about her background.[74] Miss Salvage was originally from Canterbury and attended the Presbyterian Church there for ten years as well as teaching in the Sunday School. After leaving school she worked in the Post Office before beginning her training as a deaconess at St Andrew's College, Birmingham, where she completed the Certificate of Proficiency in Religious Knowledge. She also completed a further course at Westminster College, Cheshunt.

While Kay Salvage's ordination was a significant moment in her life and the life of Crossway, it was a little overshadowed by the opening and dedication of Crossway United Reformed Church (formerly Crossway

---

[74] *Crossroads,* January 1975, Crossway United Reformed Church archives.

Central Mission) in its new building at 2:30 pm on the same day. That event was stewarded by members of Heygate Estate Tenants Association and attended by Rt Revd David Sheppard, Bishop of Woolwich, and the United Reformed Church Southern Province Moderator Vernon Lowis. The sermon was delivered by Revd Arthur Macarthur, the last general secretary of the Presbyterian Church of England (PCE) and then current moderator and general secretary of the URC. The mayor of Southwark, Mrs Margaret Georgina Farrow, had also promised to be present. Admission was by ticket only given the reduced capacity of the new building, which was only able to accommodate 150. The programme for the opening was planned as follows:

2:30   Official Party meet at St Matthew's Church for a
           brief service of thanksgiving.
3:00   Opening and Dedication of the new Building
4:30   Tea at St Matthew's Church
5:45   Reassemble at Crossway
6:00   Ordination of Miss Kay Salvage[75]

Reflecting on the events in a pastoral letter in August 1975, Revd Essex noted the length of time it took for the building to be completed and referred back to Revd Kenward who also bemoaned the late running of building works. He thanked the folk who made the events a success, naming Barry Carter, the Crossway student minister who went on to enjoy a long and much valued ministry at St Andrew's, Brockley. He spoke of his pride in the speeches made by former ministers Ronald Christopher, Stanley Boorman and Ernest Ashdown. He reminded readers that Kay Salvage was the first deaconess to be ordained since the formation of the United Reformed Church.[76] In a recent conversation between her and the author of this book, it transpired that she is the only deaconess ordained into the URC even 40 years later, as the post does not exist and is not recognised.

Miss Salvage was mainly involved in teaching and pastoral work, although she shared in other aspects of ministry, especially healing. During the evening service of 6 April 1975 people were invited to 'come

---

[75] Church Opening Service sheet, 25 January 1975, Crossway United Reformed Church archives.
[76] Ralph Essex, pastoral letter, August 1975, Crossway United Reformed Church archives.

forward' for the laying on of hands. From the 60 who attended that service, 25 came forward. It is hoped that Crossway's healing ministry will be expanded in the years to come: fast forward to 21 April 2018 and there is an event planned at the new, new Crossway entitled 'A Night of Miracle: Experience the healing ministry of Jesus'. The contemporary church also has weekly healing services.

Revd Essex catalogued the growing use of the new building and the strengthening of the ecumenical relations with St Matthew's, which had resulted in them closing their evening service and joining Crossway, increasing average attendance to between 20 and 30 people. The Girls' Brigade and Cubs restarted in the new building and the Women's fellowship was up to 60 every week. The holiday club attracted 80 children for a fortnight during the summer and the gigantic undertaking of producing *Crossroads* (a community newspaper) each month was maintained. Finances remained a struggle and were made worse by the higher costs of running the newer building and the late payment of monies owed by the council to the church. On balance the situation at this time was hopeful, and the task of evangelism was brought to the forefront of the leadership team who saw that the task of building the church had really just begun.

Revd Essex – supported by his wife Jeannie and Miss Salvage, and joined by John Cribb, a full-time member of South London Industrial Mission (SLIM), along with Rector Keith Pound and the Anglican clergy team – consolidated the work in the Elephant over the next three years until he retired on 30 July 1978. He had been 37 years in ministry, having trained at New College in London and served at Seven Kings, as a forces chaplain at the end of the Second World War, and later at Maldon, Broadway, Hammersmith, Tooting and Mitcham in addition to Crossway. He retired to St Leonards-on-Sea and died on 6 September 1993 aged 78.

The membership statistics for the period spanning Revd Boorman's ministry and Revd Essex's are shown overleaf:

Year	Minister	Membership	Children in Sunday School	Sunday School Leaders
1957	Stanley	75	250	18
1959	Boorman	48	109	10
1960		49	111	12
1961		51	127	15
1962		53	138	13
1963		54	141	14
1964	Ernest	48	141	14
1965	Ashdown	43	80	8
1966		44	80	6
1967		39	73	7
1969		34	53	7
1970	Brian Pavett	35	30	3
1971	Ralph Essex	17	35	4
1973		20	61	9
1974		20	62	8
1975		20	40	5
1977		14	40	5

Church membership statistics (1957-1977).

Peter McIntosh: 1979-1984

Peter McIntosh has been a prominent figure in the United Reformed Church during his 35 years of ministry. He joined Crossway from Byker, Priory Green, and Dartford on Friday 27 April 1979 during a service of induction that started at 7:30 pm and was presided over by the moderator of the URC Southern Province, Revd C. Cyril Franks. The charge was preached by Revd Brenda Stephenson, the minister of Charlton URC and interim moderator at Crossway. A photo of the Elephant Group of Churches, featuring Revd Angus Galbraith, Revd McIntosh, Kay Salvage, Revd John and Mrs Janet Driver and Revd John Cribb[77] was published in the next issue of *Crossroads* magazine. Alongside it, in a piece entitled 'Crossway's new minister completes team', Revd McIntosh writes:

> *Moving house, home, circumstances and schools isn't easy. But thanks to the kindness and the love of Crossway and St Matthew's churches and the welcoming of neighbours, friends and strangers, the upheaval's been coped with, and the new life begun.*[78]

Responding to the question of what it's like at the Elephant, he reflected on something once said to him.

> *You can look at a rose bush in two ways – either the hard thorns or the fragrant flower.*

So he adds:

> *I look forward to new life with you all amongst the thorns and the roses alike.*

There appears to be a gap in the archives of about two years between 1979 and 23 February 1982, when the records pick up again. The first entry indicates that the church hall had been rewired at a cost of £500. (Bearing in mind that the building had only been open for seven years this seems staggeringly soon.) In the same meeting, the church leadership also considered an extension to the building and suggested that the original design was not fit for purpose.[79]

In August 1982 it was reported that Revd Cribb would be leaving in January 1983 to return to Australia. The St Matthew's Vicarage where the Cribb family lived was due for demolition, which would also mean that Kay Salvage and Trish Belcher (who became treasurer in September 1983) would be made homeless. Alternative housing was needed and the

---

[77] Revd John Cribb had a job beyond the congregation with the South London Industrial Mission (SLIM) and was in a sense an ordained member of the church, but not a minister in the church.

[78] *Crossroads,* May 1979, Crossway United Reformed Church archives.

[79] Church Meeting minutes, 23 February 1982, Crossway United Reformed Church archives.

possibility of creating two flats at the Pilgrim building was considered. It was also reported that St Matthew's was losing their curate and therefore the leadership team of the Elephant Group of Churches was breaking up.[80]

Revd Peter McIntosh.

Patricia Wardle: 1983-1992

The first request for another church to use the Crossway building came in January 1983, but the Church Meeting decided not to allow it. (In 2018 ten congregations share Crossway's new space.) In April that year the possibility of a part-time associate minister was discussed, and it was agreed that Revd Patricia ("Pat") Wardle was to be approached. The church met Revd Wardle on 29 May 1983, and after she preached that evening the Meeting issued her a call which she accepted. Miss Salvage had in the meantime moved to Brockley to take up new work there. Revd Wardle was inducted to Crossway on Sunday 4 September 1983 at 3:00 pm with the moderator Revd Cyril Franks presiding. The charge was preached by Revd Richard J. Hall – Pat's tutor and the moderator of the General Assembly, 1976-77.

---

[80] Church Meeting minutes, August 1982, Crossway United Reformed Church archives.

In a letter written specifically for this book, Revd Wardle reflects at length on her time at the Elephant:

> [During my] first visit introduction to Pilgrim building [I] found Al-Anon [a charity] had offices on the ground floor and upstairs the space was being converted to two living spaces with a 'floating' spare room at the top of the central stairs. There was a resident cat which had belonged to the previous occupants.
>
> The two flat[s] created reasonable rents and were allocated to two church members who had lived in accommodation within St Matthew's Vicarage which was due for demolition so the tenants had been given notice to leave.
>
> The history was that this building had replaced an earlier building a little further along the road which had been damaged in the Second World War. There was considerable interest in the records there, especially from America.
>
> I remember a planned but unconfirmed visit of fifty American tourists arriving to see the records and experience the 'aura' of the area where their ancestors had lived as they were exploring their family history. After a visit to Pilgrim Church Buildings we returned to Crossway and found tea and biscuits were very welcome as the tea was in real china cups (hastily borrowed from the manse). As they were leaving I was given an envelope which contained a £50 note... the first I had ever seen.
>
> I had studied to get my Lay Preacher's certificate, then as the last person to train for ministry through the Roll of Ministers scheme I was introduced to Crossway as I had offered for part-time ministry. I had two teenagers still at home. My older children had left home. I was not the first woman to come to Crossway, sometime before there had been a husband/wife team.
>
> I 'preached with a view' on Trinity Sunday and met with the members and subsequently the ecumenical team. I remember telling the members that I was not a clever theologian but was probably OK as a pastor. This post would be to work

alongside Revd Peter McIntosh to replace Deaconess Kay Salvage who had recently moved on.

So, for a year I was half time minister and half time physiotherapist at Dulwich Hospital. After a year Peter was to move on and I put myself on the line. Crossway had to make the decision:

1. I could leave at the same time as Peter and leave the way open to call a new minister

2. Stay half time and hope that someone else would be called

3. Call me full time

I was called full time and with my teenagers I moved into the manse at the back of the church building from a home with a garden in Balham to a flat which, from the window, the wall opposite had graffiti that said, 'Don't drink and drive, take smack and fly,' quite an eye opener for teenagers.

In all the Crossway history two people were faithful stalwarts. Win (Thomas) and Kath (Hutchings) had lived in the area all their lives. First in the tenement buildings pulled down to make way for the Heygate and later in Forest Hill. They went to the old Crossway as children, Win told me that at seven years old she gave her life to Jesus and remained faithful until in her 90s. Between them they saw daughters and granddaughters come to Girls' Brigade so knew and understood the family histories, complications and dynamics.

Win and Kath, who were conscientious objectors, had been fire-watchers during the Second World War and some of their watching was from Crossway roof. Before the war Kath trained as a telephone operator and could very cleverly use her telephone voice when needed instead of her London accent.

Both of them trained as teachers after the war and this was evident in the care and teaching quietly given to those in their care. They were both kind, wise, patient, reliable and generous.

Both Win and Kath saw themselves as custodians of faith, of their home, of GB [Girls' Brigade], and of Crossway always *seeing themselves as sowers of seeds – never expecting to see the harvest.*

The new Crossway building was a nightmare with four flat roofs – very susceptible to break-ins and not friendly for funerals with the sanctuary upstairs. The new flats on the Heygate were at first little palaces as for the first time the residents had their own front door and their own bathroom. However when the flats became empty squatters moved in and the estate became less well managed.

Evening services could sometimes be eventful with various people coming and going including one eventful time when the fire alarm was set off and the secretary kept a finger on the alarm until I sawed the end off a ruler to stop the alarm ... the service continued. There were many local people who watched out for Crossway and warned of problems or odd things happening. Some of the most endearing were the people who called at the door. Usually these were people wanting a sandwich, a cup of tea and a chat. Or it may be 'Will you do the baby for me on Sunday?' (The party was already arranged on one occasion).

Although initially christened in the Church of England I was baptised in the Baptist denomination at the age of 14 but had not worked so closely with another denomination so the Anglican influence was felt strongly, both enriching and sometimes limiting. I was fortunate to be working with the rector Angus Galbraith and three curates, Geoff Annas, Andrew Davey and Jonathan Greener.

During a long Annual General Meeting in September 1983, Revd McIntosh reported that he was hopeful for the coming year, despite acknowledging that not everything was right yet and some things were still very wrong. The next big challenge was the imminent demolition of St Matthew's, but the offer to use Crossway Hall was refused and tensions were growing. The minutes record, *'Peter was glad to be a minister here and sometimes he too had had bad days when he wished he wasn't.'* The meeting ended in prayers at 9:31 p.m., nearly two hours after it started. Many of the church leaders expressed great concern about the low giving of members and the excess of expenditure over income.

Patricia Belcher is recorded as consistently urging the church and the leadership to be better stewards of the finances. (By 2009 there were nearly £500,000 held in investments at the Synod on behalf of the church as a result of the relocation of the old building, so it is strange to read these warnings and concerns.)

In a letter to Theresa the church secretary, dated May 1984, Revd McIntosh outlines his thinking about his future ministry. In addition to his work at Crossway it involved oversight responsibilities at Emmanuel East Dulwich URC and teaching within the churches of the Southern Province of the URC. As a result of conversations with the moderator, he decided to lay down the ministry at Crossway. Revd McIntosh had not just had the challenge of ministering in the area; he had also found love in the arms of Miss Salvage. They eventually married at East Dulwich on 6 December 1986. Revd McIntosh went on to become the Provincial Training Officer for the Southern Province, and served the church at Portslade and Hounsom Memorial before radically transforming the fortunes of The Windermere Centre, during which time he also served as the moderator of General Assembly. In 'retirement' he was director of Lomas House and Warden of Crowhurst Healing Centre. The couple have settled into proper retirement in Haywards Heath and were pleased to help in the compilation of this book.

There were two ministerial items on the agenda of the Church Meeting of Monday 17 September 1984. Firstly, the church was asked to decide whether they wished to call Revd Wardle full-time to the pastorate: they unanimously said yes. The other was a request from Theresa Gregory to help her discern a calling to full-time stipendiary ministry. There is no further minute on the matter specifically and no mention of her at all until 2 September 1985 when she is reported as resigning her position as secretary and Synod representative ahead of a move to Crawley where she would be taking up a new nursing post.[81]

Marion Morling: 1987-1997

In the minutes of 5 February 1987 it was reported that Crossway needed extra staff, at least part-time, mainly to help Revd Wardle with pastoral care. By 20 July the name of Marion Morling was brought to

---

[81] Church Meeting minutes, 17 September 1984, Crossway United Reformed Church archives.

the meeting. A member of Grove Centre, Sydenham, she felt called to inner-city ministry. The church meeting called her to serve part-time from 1 October 1987.[82]

The question of letting the Crossway building to another church was fully discussed in the meeting on 7 January 1990 following a request from a New Testament Church which wanted to use the hall for two-and-a-half hours on a Thursday evening. Many voiced their misgivings because of stories they had heard about unruly behaviour in other churches. Guided by Revd Wardle the group was given permission to start Bible studies and prayers meeting. On 29 April 1990 concern over a Nigerian wedding let was expressed. Evidently the children who attended were unsupervised and created a lot of mess. It was suggested that the church should not allow receptions, only services. Instead of accepting this proposal, the decision was taken to triple the fee from £50 to £150 to cover the cost of cleaning and reparation. In July 1990 a litany of damage and costs incurred was submitted to one church user, Wilfred, after his wedding blessing and reception – clearly the permission to allow parties in the church building was not working.[83]

At the AGM on 25 April 1991 the name of Margaret Collins was brought before the meeting as someone wishing to be linked to Crossway for one year to gain inner-city experience as part of her non-stipendiary ministry.

The challenge of holding onto the team ministry and looking after Crossway was taking its toll on Revd Wardle, and led to her asking for a vote of confidence during the meeting held on 13 June 1991. Win Thomas chaired this part of the meeting and it was recorded that *'in many and varied ways, love and concern was expressed for Pat, and an eagerness that she be affirmed in what she has struggled for. We wish Pat to lead us into our new venture.'*[84]

[82] Church Meeting minutes, 5 February 1987, Crossway United Reformed Church archives.

[83] Church meeting minutes, 29 April 1990, Crossway United Reformed Church archives.

[84] Church Meeting minutes, 13 June 1990, Crossway United Reformed Church archives.

Jim Gould: 1993-2003

There is another gap in the minutes at this point, and they jump to 18 January 1996 when Revd J. Gould is in the chair. From yearbooks we can establish that Revd Wardle retired to North Shields in 1992 where she was joined by her friend and companion Trish Belcher, the Crossway treasurer. There is no record of Revd Gould's induction but the yearbook shows that he was trained at Mansfield College, Oxford, and served as Minister in Feltham and Twyford & Woodley before coming to Crossway in 1993.[85]

Unemployment on the Heygate Estate was high at the time and there were many social problems. A URC Bromley District Council visitation report from January 1996 voices concern that during the excellent meal they enjoyed with the church leadership in the manse dining room, they were disturbed several times by things being thrown at the windows from the walkway. The visitors were even more concerned that this was so readily accepted by the minister. The estate was reported to suffer from vandalism and it was known to have its share of drug abuse and trafficking, car theft, burglaries and arson. In the words of the minister, many of the people living on the estate *come in at night, lock their steel security doors and dream of the day when they can move to Sidcup'*. The report concludes:

> *We were impressed by the nature and quality of the work that is being done at Crossway. The church seems to be in good heart, spiritually vibrant and coping admirably with the many challenges of life in the inner city. The Minister seems very much to be the right man in the right place, and under his leadership the whole church exercises Christ's Ministry to the community it serves. We hope that all the churches of the District will keep Crossway U.R.C. in their prayers.[86]*

Marion Morling left Crossway at the end of 1997 and there was a farewell event at Christ Church and Upton Chapel on 3 January 1998. Somewhere between the meetings of 21 May and 18 June 1998 it was confirmed that Barbara Caley, who had been the church administrator for some time, was to cease continuing in that role. The minute simply

---

[85] United Reformed Church yearbooks, 1972, Dr Williams's Library, London.
[86] URC Bromley District visitation report, January 1996, Crossway United Reformed Church archives.

says that Jim (Revd Gould) spoke of the church's sadness at Barbara's leaving. Maureen Jackson took over the captaincy of Girls' Brigade (GB) on 5 April 1998. (In 2018 Barbara Caley continues to attend GB which is now under the leadership of Mandy Buckberry, Maureen Jackson's daughter.) The position of administrator was taken up by Allyson White who began work on 1 July 1998. The minutes are not precise but nevertheless clearly indicate that Revd Gould married Cathy in the summer of 1998, as a reference to a hiccup over the honeymoon accommodation caused much hilarity.[87]

By this point Southwark Council was again thinking about redeveloping the Heygate Estate. A minute from the meeting held on 21 January 1999 indicates that Revd Gould sought to enlighten those in attendance about timetables and current council thinking regarding the estate and the church. He presented possible options for consideration and suggested that Crossway have a day away to think, pray and plan for the future.

Allyson White tendered her resignation with effect from 29 February 2000 because she and her retired husband were unable to secure affordable accommodation in London. Her role was taken up by Gillian Webb from 4 April 2000.

Reading through the minutes of Revd Gould's ministry it is evident that he was able to bring stability to the church. Month after month the same people attended the church meetings and with the strong and accurate leadership of Gillian Webb as administrator, the fabric and management of the plant was wonderfully looked after. Revd Gould took on an impressive monthly diet of work and clearly controlled the vision and outlook of the congregation. His new wife Cathy played a full role in the church taking on a great deal of pastoral care. On 13 February 2003 Revd Gould announced that he had accepted a call to 'The Hyde', Colindale and was to be inducted to the pastorate on 20 September. In the same meeting and (nowadays) quite unusually he spoke of a possible candidate to take his place: Revd Robin Pagan. Due process arrangements were made for his induction service on 20 September 2003.[88]

---

[87]   Church Meeting minutes, September 1998, Crossway United Reformed Church archives.
[88]   Church Meeting minutes, 13 February 2003, Crossway United Reformed Church archives.

Robin Pagan: 2003-2004

Revd Pagan responded to a request for an article reflecting his time at Crossway as follows:

My first real involvement with Crossway was when I accompanied them on their annual youth trip with Rev Jim Gould in charge. This was done in conjunction with St Matthew's. We went to Thorpe Park and my main impression was one of relief that we got them all back in one piece. On the second occasion I was responsible for their wellbeing so a visit to Whipsnade Zoo had its challenges. One thing I remember was a teenage girl who spent most of her time in the sand pit enjoying the sand in her toes. A case of urban sensory deprivation?

But the real youth contribution which ran throughout the year was the Girl's Brigade group run by Maureen Jackson. At that time there was a trend within the wider church to be somewhat critical of uniformed organisations and I confess that I have never been a great enthusiast of them but I did recognise that the work that Maureen did with the girls and the structure the organisation gave were invaluable to their formation and self development. I did what I could to encourage them.

The ecumenical relationship with St Matthew's was somewhat nominal (summer youth trips excluded). Even the joint monthly newsletter wasn't really that joint anymore. However my relationship with Rev Neil McKinnon was a good one. His early visit to welcome me with a bottle of bubbly got things off to a good start and should be recommended on all ecumenical ministerial training programmes (check alcohol issues in advance).

There were no 'Royal Connections' in my short time at Crossway but Neil did share with me his Princess Diana experience when she had visited some years earlier. More than once, he was quite smitten.

The local Council of Churches was quite conscientious in its meetings but I don't remember it getting up to anything too exciting.

Living in the manse at Crossway was quite an experience. When my wife and I went for a preliminary look around Jim introduced us to some of its peculiarities. One being the windows which he kept open with half a tennis ball and wouldn't close properly. This put us into something of a dilemma as we were under the impression that the whole site was soon to be redeveloped. However, we had to ask for the place to be properly secured and the church obliged. As it happens the redevelopment was delayed and I assume the reglazing made its contribution to the comfort of my successors. Once I became used to the place I never felt under any great threat to my safety and when dubious figures were seen dashing around the walkways outside the 1st floor windows they were usually accompanied by a film crew making their latest gritty number. On one occasion I left my car on the pavement outside the front door which was on church property only to find that it had [been] taken to the Car Pound in New Kent Road. A bus journey and 100 pound fine later I had it back. I eventually got the fine refunded with the help of a local councillor.

Living in the church buildings had its drawbacks. On one Sunday morning the door duty person was late and I was reprimanded by those waiting to get in: 'It's your house, why haven't you opened the door?' On the other hand my Sunday afternoon washing up sessions at the sink were accompanied by the Ghanaian church's singing in the church proper as they used it for their worship sessions. I have to confess that I was somewhat autocratic in my re-disposition of church furnishing and hangings. In particular I had the hangings based on the GNB [Good News Bible] illustrations by Maureen hung in the church. She had a real gift and I think they were an improvement on the originals. I wonder where they are now, or if they are?

I was impressed and interested by the historic connections we had through the Dover Street buildings but could never find ways to involve the church in that history. As to the building itself, it seemed to run along on its own steam and I was not there long enough to effect any substantial or useful changes. As to the congregation itself I felt the morning worship successfully integrated the traditional white community and the mainly African (Ghanaian) recent arrivals. The evening service was more the preserve of the old timers with Win and Kath in regular attendance who told me how close they had been to closure but through persistence and prayer had once again arisen. Long may it be so. One of my efforts to contribute to the integration of the two communities was to form a group of elders from each of them and this group met regularly on several occasions before I had to move on due to my daughter's ill health at the time.[89]

Steve Titus: 2006-2007

Revd Pagan's ministry was shortened because of family needs and he went to Norfolk to conclude his ministerial career. Revd Sue Powell was appointed by the Synod to act as interim moderator during the vacancy. The Synod decided to recruit via the Council for World Mission and called Revd Steve Titus, former president of the United Congregational Church of Southern Africa. His service of induction was set for 14 May 2006 at 4:00 p.m. He had visited the entire congregation within three months and introduced more formality to the morning worship as requested by the Ghanaian members of the congregation. A six-month review under the Mission Partnership Exchange Scheme was carried out and concerns about Revd Titus's ministry were expressed. He took these and a number of health concerns into account and decided to return to South Africa in May 2007 resulting in yet another vacancy at Crossway, the fourth in four years. Revd Bryn Thomas was invited to serve as interim minister initially for one year. He was invited to preach on 17 June 2007.

---

[89] Email communication from Robin Pagan to the author, 6 September 2017.

Bryn Thomas: 2007-2009

The church was facing the prospect of another redevelopment and membership numbers had plummeted, especially as some members felt that Revd Titus had been treated shamefully and left in protest. One of the few constants that remained was the leadership of the administrator Gill Webb who also acted as pastoral carer and maintenance coordinator. This was not to last: Gill resigned her post around March 2008 after satisfactorily completing the previous year's accounts.

The church benefitted during this period by a new dynamic presence at Crossway, Mr Tim Reith, who shared many ideas. His charismatic enthusiasm resulted in the formation of a student ministry team and the appointment of a youth worker part-funded by Synod grants. In the background, concern was growing about the church property at Great Dover Street (the old Pilgrim Fathers' Memorial Chapel building) and a sensitive situation relating to the two tenants. A couple (who were not related to the church) occupied the larger space, while a family with three children was crammed into two bedrooms. The situation was further complicated by the fact that the mother of the family was a long-time and much respected member of Crossway church. It was decided to evict the couple. Revd Thomas had been presented with a 'hornet's nest' that he was going to have to prod!

Mrs Irene Gondwe, a member of the congregation from Malawi, temporarily took control of the church administration in 2008 and Mr Reith continued to bombard the church with creative and innovative ideas. Meanwhile, Revd Thomas slowly fell in love with the church secretary Sue Moinzadeh: they eventually married in 2009. Interestingly there is no announcement of the marriage in the minutes, just a change of name to Sue Thomas.

Peter Stevenson: 2009-present

One of Mr Reith's ideas was to encourage the Synod to apply for a Special Category Minister from Church House, arguing that the plans for regeneration of the Elephant and Castle and the further redevelopment of Crossway would require a dedicated and focussed ministry.

Revd Peter Stevenson visited the vacancy group in March 2009, and it was reported that initial reactions to him were positive: he was described as 'brilliant', 'down-to-earth', 'easy to relate to', 'feet on the ground' and 'head and heart'. He was invited to preach with a view on 3

May 2009. The minutes of 19 May indicate that Revd Stevenson had been called by 100 per cent of the membership and he would now be inheriting the 'hornet's nest'. He arrived on Bank Holiday Monday, 31 August 2009, to a cockroach-infested manse without Dawn his wife, and immediately set about discovering the many challenges that were to be unearthed.[90]

---

[90] Church Meeting minutes, March 2009, Crossway United Reformed Church archives.

CHAPTER FIVE

Local Ecumenical Project

CROSSWAY CENTRAL MISSION HAS ALWAYS WORKED HARD to encourage collaboration with other churches in the area, recognising that while God's people can work well as individuals, they can achieve amazing things when they work together. In the 1960s and '70s, Crossway worked particularly closely with St Matthew's Church of England, Holy Trinity Church of England, and the Pilgrim Fathers' Memorial Church (an independent fellowship that became part of the London Congregational Union in 1964). Collectively, they were known as the Elephant Group.

A document entitled 'Report of the Group to consider setting up an area of Ecumenical Experiment', dated 1 October 1972, shows how the group believed that God was guiding them to link into one Christian Fellowship for a variety of reasons:

1. *to provide an efficient structure for the sharing in Christ's mission for all aspects of life in this area and to undergird this with necessary prayer and worship;*

2. *to be free to experiment, to discover ways of meeting the needs of the area and to work with others who are doing this;*

3. *to make it possible for each member of the Church, under God, to bring his or her personal contribution and to make the best use of our resources and*

4. *to demonstrate our common aim and to show the unity and diversity which can exist in one church.*[91]

---

[91] 'Report of the Group to consider setting up an area of Ecumenical Experiment', 1 October 1972, Crossway United Reformed Church archives.

The background information in the Ecumenical Experiment report explained that...

> *St Matthew and Crossway have worked together and shared in joint acts of worship over a long period. Since 1969 children's work has been shared. Since the summer of 1970 all services for the Anglicans and the Crossway have taken place in St Matthew's Church. Early in the same year combined weekly staff meetings were begun. Since October of 1971 the team has been responsible for the services at the Pilgrim Fathers' Church which is now formally part of Crossway United Reformed Church. The arrival of Mr Essex in November 1972 meant that again there was a full time Congregationalist (now United Reformed) minister as a member of the ministerial team.[92]*

It is clear that the demolition of the old Crossway building precipitated a drive towards ecumenical unity, and the respect Revds Keith Pound, Pavett and Essex had for each other is evident in their respective fellowship letters of September 1971 and Easter 1972.[93]

Revd Essex's report on the opening of the new Crossway building three years later, in August 1975, indicates that the ecumenical drive and excitement persisted. He reports:

> *We began the proceedings with a service of thanksgiving in St Matthew's Church conducted by the Rt Rev. David Sheppard, then Bishop of Woolwich. In that service we remembered before God with gratitude all that we shared in that building, and prayed that the opening of the new building would not divide us. It is much harder to be one with two buildings but we are trying.*

During the reception the Bishop was heard to say that the *'partnership between St Matthew and Crossway must continue'*. Revd Essex's account continues:

---

[92]   *Ibid.*
[93]   In his first pastoral letter to Crossway in Easter 1972, Revd Essex gives special thanks to Revd Pound and Revd Pavett for their warm welcome and support.

Since Crossway opened St Matthew's have closed their evening service and join with us every Sunday at 6:30. On occasions they have also held the Parish Communion at Crossway instead of at St Matthew's on Sunday mornings when we have con-celebrated. I cannot tell you what a help and encouragement this has been to us and I am well aware that this has meant a considerable sacrifice on the part of our Anglican friends ... Our involvement in the Parish of 9,000 people in conjunction with St Matthew's continues. At the moment the Children's Summer Holiday Project when we look after 80 children for a fortnight is in progress. A gigantic undertaking each month is the production of Crossroads, *an 8-page newspaper which reads more like a community newspaper, which is what it is meant to be, rather than a church magazine.*[94]

A visitation report of summer 1976 written by Revd D.J.D. Baker claims that...

The key to the new Crossway is its joint work with the neighbouring Anglican Church in the wider area of estates and the willingness of the URC to maintain its commitment there.[95]

During the displacement of Crossway, a ministry team of the Anglican rector, the URC minister, appointees by the Diocese of Southwark and Bromley District of Thames South Province of URC, together with a lay person from both denominations acted as the governing council responsible for the day-to-day running of the churches. In spring 1978 the Crossway management committee chairman reported that Revd Ralph Essex would be retiring in July after six years' ministry at Crossway. On 8 November that year the Anglican Archdeacon Revd Michael Whinney wrote to the Bishop of Southwark about the appointment of a new incumbent at Holy Trinity with St Matthew's

---

[94] Ralph Essex, report on the opening of the new Crossway, August 1975, Crossway United Reformed Church archives.
[95] URC Bromley District visitation report, Summer 1976, Crossway United Reformed Church archives.

Southwark and the United Reformed Minister at Crossway, pointing out that...

> *These two churches although not having a formalised a legal sharing agreement nevertheless have for many years been working very closely together as a team with joint staff meetings, joint services and a joint approach to many aspects of their congregational and parish life. Consequently when you put forward the name of the Rev. Angus Galbraith to be the new incumbent, arrangements were made for the URC District representative to meet him as a matter of courtesy and consultation together. You delayed your announcement of this appointment until we had heard from the URC representatives that they were as equally delighted as the Anglican parish.*
>
> *The URC church has reciprocated by inviting me as your representative to meet the proposed URC minister for Crossway before his appointment was ratified and this I have done today along with Angus Galbraith, the incoming incumbent. We were very pleased with the new man proposed and said that we were happy to have been consulted and would of course be delighted with him in the future.[96]*

The 'new man proposed' was Revd Peter E. McIntosh, who was inducted to the Crossway United Reformed Church (with St Matthew's) Elephant Group of Churches on Friday 27 April 1979.

Revd Angus Galbraith became involved through his own conversations with the Anglican diocese regarding the redevelopment of St Matthew's church. It had been suggested that the folk there join Crossway and use the new building for their worship. He laid out the reasons why this would not work, pointing to the (lack of?) historical connection to the area; the barrier of the New Kent Road which fell between the two churches; and the congregation of St Matthew's being against it. Perhaps most illuminating is his first reason:

> *Key to my whole pastoral strategy is the creation of a place of prayer where the Eucharist can be celebrated daily with the use of colour, drama and symbols, and where there is the right*

---

[96] Anglican Archdeacon Revd Michael Whinney, letter to the Bishop of Southwark, 8 November 1978.

atmosphere for other types of worship. I want our worship to be simple but beautiful, and meditative and accessible in style, where people feel at home. The blessed sacrament icons and a place to light candles will all be part of this. In no way could that be incorporated into Crossway Church without losing the right setting for our joint Sunday evening worship and the insights that the URC church have to teach us. We all want the riches of both traditions, and not something which springs from the lowest common denominator. That, I believe, is by far the most important reason.[97]

A meeting of the Elephant Churches was held at Crossway on 11 June 1984. Under the heading 'Local Ecumenical Project' the minutes from the time read:

The pros and cons of an LEP were again considered. In view of the clear understanding between the two Churches shown in the reports of the Team Days Away, and the entirely satisfactory working relationship, it was agreed there was no reason to pursue the formalities of entering into an LEP.

By this time Revd McIntosh had resigned his post at Crossway, and Revd Wardle, while formally serving part-time, had increased her deployment to full-time in order to lead the Crossway team. It may be too extreme to suggest that cracks in the unofficial LEP were showing at this point, but a minute under the heading 'Membership of Elephant Churches' indicates some tension:

Angus [Galbraith] and Pat [Wardle] said they had together started looking at their joint concerns relating to membership of either Church: it would be useful to air them. There might be existing members who would waver in their allegiances to one Church or the other, and new people who became involved on both sides of the Road and who at some stage would want to decide where to make their commitment. There

---

[97] Angus Galbraith, correspondence in the Crossway United Reformed Church archives.

would need to be much sensitivity and understanding in such cases. They would try to get their thoughts on to paper.[98]

Other meetings on this topic did take place (dates were fixed for 10 June and 9 December 1985) but the minutes for them are not available. However, the next part of the story is glimpsed in the minutes of the St Matthew's & Crossway Advisory Group (it is interesting to see how the name of this group changed over the years) dated 26 June 1991. By this point each church conducted their own meetings separately each week, and they only came together once per month as one team. Perhaps the most poignant entry is found under the heading 'Development of relationship between the Churches':

Pat described how we had become aware at Team Days Away of how much we had changed in the years of the partnership and how St Matthew's proposed move out of their premises had caused a lot of re-thinking on both sides of the road. We had given thought to the things we do well together and those that we do not. Tricia (Miss Belcher) reminded us of the enormous change in the congregations in the last twenty years. Angus said that there was now very little cross-filtration in each other's worship. He commented on Tricia's remarks at Team Days Away that St Matthew's had moved 'higher' in their form of worship while Crossway had moved 'lower'.

The minutes record a lengthy conversation in the group that shows how far apart the congregations had drifted.[99]

However, this may not tell the full story. A letter dated 24 June 1991 (two days prior to the Advisory Group meeting) seems to suggest that a Parochial Church Council (PCC) of 4 June had already indicated that St Matthew's would not move to the Crossway site while their building was redeveloped. A subsequent PCC the following year, on 4 October 1992, adopted a resolution to that effect:

That as from 10th October 1992, the formal non legal agreement between Crossway U.R.C. and St Matthew's Church, concerning their ecumenical relationship and which

---

[98] Minutes of a meeting involving the Elephant churches, 11 June 1984, Crossway United Reformed Church archives.
[99] Minutes of the St Matthew's & Crossway Advisory Group, 26 June 1991.

was recognised by the United Reformed Church and the Church of England, be terminated. As such the Advisory Committee would cease to meet. This would also release both congregations from all previous agreements including consultations on the appointment of a minister or priest.[100]

It looks as though Crossway actually ended the relationship two days earlier. In a letter dated 16 November 1992, J. Michael Rees thanks Revd Welby for her letter that included minutes of the Crossway Church Meeting held on Thursday 8 October 1992…

…where you record under item 6, the unanimous acceptance of the resolution terminating the formal non-legal agreement between Crossway URC and St Matthew's Church of England.[101]

It matters little who 'chucked' who but it is sad that 25 years or more of ecumenical working together came to such an end. In an interview with Revd Peter McIntosh for this book, he revealed his belief that the clergy team had become too large and disabled the laity.[102] By 1996 the church meeting minutes do not make any reference to ecumenical work with the exception of the Holiday Project, which continued, and joint-led Christmas services.

Revd Angus Galbraith was also interviewed for this book, and later sent an email detailing the fantastic work that had resulted from the close partnership of the clergy teams. St Matthew's church was closely linked with the South Western Theological College which sent students to the Elephant under the auspices of an Urban Engagement Programme. Each year, young ordinands would be set tasks and projects to achieve, and as a result the clergy team was continually enriched. Some found the experience of working with the Free Church easier than others, but all were challenged to reflect on their own theological thinking and ecclesiological preferences. Revd Galbraith also had a number of curates under his tutelage. The parish had a 'spare' rectory and many of the clergy team lived in intentional community during this period. It is worth quoting Revd Galbraith at length about this period, to understand his

---

[100] St Matthew's PCC Meeting minutes, 4 October 1992.
[101] Crossway URC letter to URC District council, 8 October 1992.
[102] Peter McIntosh, interview with the author, 4 October 2017.

role and motivations, and to get an overview of the changes taking place at Crossway at the time:

I know my curates will have had something to do with the relationship between the two churches. I inherited for about a year the Revd John Driver. He was married to Janet, who I think at the time worked for CMS. They were very fond of Ralph Essex and were very pro the relationship with Crossway, as indeed was Malcolm Torry who followed. Geoff Annas was next and I think he worked well with Pat Wardle. Geoff's commitment to Crossway was practical and he had a liberal theological background. Andrew Davey followed on and he was very keen on social justice issues and I found him very theologically stimulating. He was keen on liturgy and happy to experiment. He went on to St Luke's Camberwell and after 5 years there worked in Church House on things like Faith in the City etc. He now has a parish in Tooting. I think he was less comfortable with Crossway although he took part in all the things we did together. He was trained at Westcott House.

My last curate was Jonathan Greener who is now Dean of Exeter Cathedral. He was trained at Mirfield and extremely bright, and an excellent preacher. From a more wealthy background, but really got stuck in and learnt a lot from his time at the Elephant. He was from an Anglo-Catholic background and extremely competent. The Salisbury and Wells theological college inner city training scheme terminated while he was with us. But that was in a way convenient as he took over a lot of the parish responsibilities during the planning and development of the new St Matthew's.

It was during this time that St Matthew's congregation worshipped for about a year in Crossway Hall for the Sunday morning Eucharist. Previous to that we had worshipped in the St Matthew's Hall for five years. We learnt a lot from that liturgically – free to move things around etc. It was because the parish owned the hall and I had the freehold, that any redevelopment could not just be forced on us by the diocese.

Throughout my time, I always worshipped in Crossway Sunday evening and took my part in preaching and taking the service in a way that I hope was acceptable.

Pat and Tricia were very involved in a walking group which involved people from both churches, as was Andrew Dalby who was St Matthew's treasurer and Margaret Beattie who trained and was ordained as a non-stipendiary priest while at St Matthew's. Another member was Revd Anthony Hurst. His links first started with us at the Wednesday lunchtime Eucharist with lunch afterwards. He worked nearby. He started training for the non-stipendiary priesthood at his local church and then was transferred to us. It was more a diocesan convenience placement as he had many irons in the fire on a diocesan level. In retrospect I think I could have used his gifts more, but he lived in Pimlico and so in one way was a bit detached from the Elephant. He was sometimes with us on a Sunday and sometimes preached and presided.

John Cribb, Anthony Hawley the priest at Charterhouse and myself took a pilgrimage to Taize in two minibuses. Supporting Christian Aid, especially in Christian Aid week was very much a commitment of both churches, long before I was on the scene. Each year we put a note and envelope through one third of the flats by rotation and then go to collect.

I mentioned Crossroads *newspaper. It is amazing it continued for as long as it did. It totally depended on members of both churches. At the end for my last year we replaced it with a folded sheet of A3 printed with photos and local information/ news. This went to every flat in the parish but was free. I think it stopped after that.*

Peter McIntosh started a drama group with some folk from Sunday evening worship. I steered well clear of the group which had several single women who would have liked to have been married. I have gone on far too long. I don't often think about Elephant days, although I think we had something very special there.

On my arrival [at Crossway] I inherited a scheme whereby both churches together used to visit Guy's Hospital every week. We aimed to see everyone there who lived in the parish and was in the hospital. From the records department we used to go through the sheets of everyone there and identify those to be visited. This was something the two churches did together. It took the whole of Friday afternoon. We started with prayer and did half the visiting and then met up again with a cup of tea and then did the second bit. It was a useful way of training curates to do that sort of pastoral visiting. This developed and we trained some lay people to be involved as well.

Unfortunately the plug was pulled on the whole scheme when we invited the chaplain to help with the training. It was at this time that confidentiality was becoming a big thing and we were forced to stop. It was very sad as local people really liked to be visited by people who lived in the parish and knew their block etc. The team visited far more people each week than the chaplain himself. We were there for the patients and sometimes staff would call for our assistance because we were there on the ward.

I [also] inherited a card index scheme, where there was a card for every flat and house in the parish. The council used to give us each week a list of new tenants so the cards were always (in theory) up to date. Every new arrival was visited and given a free copy of Crossroads. *But again the council at some point said they couldn't give us the info. Other details on the cards included dates of pastoral visits, whether they took* Crossroads, *baptisms, etc. This may have been fine when there was a secretary each morning and 2 curates etc. – but the cards were not really used very much and proved too onerous to keep up. They were quite useful if you were trying to write a 'Down your Way' article for* Crossroads. *It was good to start off with a few friendly visits. Both churches contributed to the system.*

Lent groups and the Holy Week Liturgy were very important to me. We encouraged as many people as possible to take part in the weekly Lent Groups, which met in people's homes. There used to be about 5 groups. One Palm Sunday we got a donkey to lead the procession into church. It came with loads of kids through the underpass at the Elephant and much to the kids' delight shat on the way. On Maundy Thursday the house groups had a Passover meal together in each of the hosts' flats then afterwards all met in Church for the Service of the Institution of the Eucharist. In one of those Pat and Tricia did a slide presentation for the intercessions and then during the Eucharistic prayer they played 'Koln Nidrie' as a background. It was very powerful. Then after that service there was an all night vigil through to Good Friday. The church never had less than two or three through the night. The vigil finished at 9am when there was the Liturgy of the Cross with veneration. Then 12 - 3pm was at Crossway with drama, a procession of witness and buns afterwards. Different things different years. At St Matthew's we did the first Eucharist of Easter at midnight, starting with the bonfire outside the church with the lighting of the paschal candle, the procession into the darkened church. And then the vigil of readings tracing the Scriptural story of redemption etc. I believe that using all our senses in a dramatic liturgy is a wonderful way of interiorising the faith.

Eating together, praying together, being together in human sized groups is I believe an important way how we grow in the faith. Hence the pilgrimages, the house/flat holy communion each week, weekly lunchtime eucharist, daily Evening Prayer in church, daily morning prayer in Rectory chapel, taking people away for the weekend to places like Michlepage Farm, Saturday trips to the seaside, people entertaining students in their flat, team tea after the hospital visiting etc. If people were sick at home we used to take a group of 3/4 to anoint and give Holy Communion with everyone joining in the laying on of hands. Polly Knight was a church warden at St Matthew's for many years and when she retired she was almost like a full time lay deacon. In the Sunday Eucharist we had several people who acted as lay deacon and stood with the president *behind the altar in addition to reading the Gospel. There was a rota for the intercessions led by lay people.*[103]

We can reflect that during their time together, Crossway and St Matthew's did some remarkable work in connecting with the local community. They should be applauded for the ministry that they led at a time of redevelopment and change. Families were ministered to and worship was offered, prayers were said and lives were impacted. Both churches were undergoing redevelopment of their own buildings and economic pressures were hampering their ability to continue the programmes they had once offered. But once the initial ecumenical fervour for structural unity had calmed, the reality – that these were two very different churches, both theologically and ecclesiologically – had to be accepted. Perhaps apathy set in, making a 'divorce' an easier option than the alternative.

By 2009, when the author of the book arrived at Crossway, the only connection between Crossway and the other local churches was the Christmas Eve service where the URC minister was invited to preach the Word at the Midnight Eucharist. He duly did so that year, but was only accompanied by his own family and none of the Crossway congregation attended. He did not preach at the 2010 service.

New collaborations

That chapter in the life of Crossway had closed, but the church is now exploring a new form of joint working. Under Revd Jim Gould (1993-2003) an increasing number of majority black churches requested space in the new building.[104] After due consideration at church meetings, and probably for financial reasons, Crossway became a home for other congregations. There has always been a need and a willingness to make the Crossway building available to others, but the idea to welcome other congregations as part of the church mission was new. Locally the majority black church demand for space to worship was growing and some took the risk to use buildings that were not fit for purpose. Southwark Council became increasingly concerned and began commissioning reports on the situation.

---

[103] Angus Galbraith, email communication to the author, 20 November 2017.
[104] See Chapter 9 for more details about the current site.

Revd Dr Peter Stevenson arrived in August 2009, the sixth minister in five years, and soon recognised that Crossway could be intentional about hosting other congregations, thus preventing some of them from moving into inappropriate structures. A later report from 2013 includes a case study of the outreach that Crossway offered. It reports that, *'Peter sees "building church" as about building worshipping communities within the building drawing on the model of a Christian Centre.'*[105] The report also records a statement by the lead pastor of the Elephant and Castle Seventh Day Adventist Church, one of the churches that were able to meet in Crossway's building:

> *[He] spoke of the struggle they had to find suitable premises, of sharp practice through last minute inflating of prices, of the difficulty of 'being overstretched' and finding 'something that's affordable'. While not avoiding the ongoing limitations of renting, when they finally came to Crossway, Pastor Kwabena said 'it is like [a] sister church, we are brothers', and remembered that 'all churches that worship here came together and had fellowship' at the joint service. Regarding engagement with the local community, 'most of the things we do share with Peter'.*[106]

This work of new ecumenism came under threat when Southwark Council announced plans to redevelop the Heygate Estate in 2006. Until then the redevelopment plan had seemed largely talk, and a global financial crisis in 2008 had delayed plans still further. But after the local elections of 6 May 2010 the new Labour-controlled authority was keen to restart negotiations with the developer Lendlease. Soon after, a 'Heads of Terms' agreement was signed between the developer and the council, and the church was forced to enter into compulsory purchase negotiations with the council. A more detailed discussion of this phase in the life follows in Chapter 9. Suffice to say that, rather than close the church, it was agreed that it should be re-provided, prompting Councillor Fiona Colley to say:

> *I am delighted that rather than simply buying out the Church, we have instead taken the decision to relocate this important*

---

[105] 'Being Built Together: Final Report' (London, University of Roehampton, June 2013), p. 91.
[106] *Ibid.*

community facility to a new purpose built church at the heart of Elephant and Castle ... Crossway [will] not only provide space for their own congregation to worship, but seek to maximise the use of their premises by other local community organisations, including eight other faith groups.[107]

At the time of writing in January 2018, ten congregations are using the Crossway building. It is home to worshippers from Brazil, Latin America, Ghana, wider western Africa, Ethiopia and the international congregation of Crossway itself.

Ecumenism, like many church initiatives, is constantly changing. Crossway Christian Centre today offers new ways of working together as God's one Church. It had been hoped that leaders of each congregation using the building would sign up to a Declaration of Missional Intent, recognising particular worship styles but committing to collective outreach and evangelism. At the time of writing it remains an aspiration.

The current collaborations continue the work of the church leaders of the 1960s and '70s. But today we must recognise that a different way of working has to be found if the Church is to remain relevant to the community and able to speak to the concerns and challenges that those in the community face.

---

[107] *Ibid.*

CHAPTER SIX

The Rich and Famous

IT IS A SHAME THAT A COMPREHENSIVE ARCHIVE DOES NOT exist for Crossway as there are occasions when people contact the church to track down a story of a loved one or a situation connected with their family. For instance, David Cameron Dudley got in touch on 23 January 2013 by email to write:

Hi!

I stumbled across something that you may find (slightly) fascinating.

I have a book that was presented to my grandfather in 1913 by the 'Crossway Brotherhood'. I know this because there is a moderately ornate printed label stuck to the front page. It reads:

CROSSWAY BROTHERHOOD

Mr A. Dudley has fulfilled the condition upon which this presentation, during the half year ending Mar 30 1913

HEBERT KENWARD	*President*
FRED A ROLFE	*Hon Sec*
G. WISE	
A.C. WEAVERS	*Registrars*

Crossway Central Mission
New Kent Road
SE

The book is a novel published in 1903 called 'Condemned as a Nihilist' by G A Henty. I wonder what my grandfather's (Alfred) connection[s] with the church were and what the conditions he fulfilled for six month[s were] in order to deserve this presentation!

The book has been sat on the bookshelf in my house (Wimbledon – where I've lived on and off since 1957) and [I] recently decided to read it! That's when I saw the label.[108]

David and his grandfather Alfred may not be rich or famous, but their connection with Crossway makes them very special. In this chapter we will discover some of the most well-known men and women who have supported Crossway, from members of the royal family to famous actors and others who could be considered rich (maybe) and famous (definitely) in their world.

The support of a Queen

It has long been suggested that Crossway once enjoyed royal patronage, but the exact details of this association have proven difficult to establish. In a letter dated 2 August 2013 to the archivist at Buckingham Palace, Revd Stevenson asked whether a royal visit to Crossway Mission had taken place in 1918. The subsequent correspondence revealed that there was a record in the Court Circular suggesting that Queen Mary visited Crossway Mission Church on 5 December 1917, accompanied by Princess Mary and Lady Mary Trefusis. The Royal Archivist went onto the say that, unfortunately, not many of Queen Mary's official papers concerning her engagements, patronages etc. have survived, making it difficult to confirm Her Majesty's activities on that day. At their suggestion, the prominent and respected Southwark historian Stephen Humphrey was contacted on 21 August 2013. He replied as follows:

The date of the event seems unusual to me for Queen Mary to make a visit without King George V, although in this case she may have been accompanied by her daughter. All the visits that she made on her own that I can recollect took place when she was a widow. This one may well have been connected with the war.

The advice from the Royal Archives to consult local newspapers is certainly the most obvious recommendation to

---

[108] David Cameron Dudley, email to Peter Stevenson, 23 January 2013.

make, and I am sure that there would be reports of a local visit by the Queen in 1917. They could be consulted at the local history library; it would be advisable to ring there first to reserve the microfilm reader.

Crossway was one of the most important churches of the wider Congregational Church in 1917. It is possible that a report would have been made in a magazine of the Congregational denomination – enquire at Dr Williams's Library, Gordon Square, for available titles – and also you could check whether magazines survey from the New Kent Road mission itself. I do not remember them from the local history library, but that does not mean that they do not exist elsewhere.

I take the opportunity to send leaflets about my new book on the Elephant and Castle. Crossway does get a passing mention or two, but my definition of the Elephant and Castle is very tight, and Crossway is being saved up for a later book on the New Kent Road and Old Kent Road.

Sadly, Mr Humphrey died of a heart attack on 30 November 2016. The book was never written.

Research for this book turned up two references to Queen Mary in Revd Boorman's contributions to the *Crossway Chronicles* of Easter 1960 and February 1961. In the 1960 edition, Boorman writes:

Our Christmas season was a joyous one and our only problem then was to arrange for so many visits to distribute to old and lonely folk the gifts that a great number of friends had made available. Each year included in such gifts is a parcel of food from H.R.H. the Princess Royal who continues the interest that her mother, Queen Mary, had in Crossway for many years. We are grateful to the Princess Mary, Princess Royal for this continued interest.[109]

---

[109] *Crossway Chronicle,* Easter 1960, Crossway United Reformed Church archives.

A year later Revd Boorman writes:

We have thanked all those who thought of our needs over Christmas, and many did think of us, we had gifts of food, including the usual very substantial parcel from H.R.H. the Princess Royal, and clothes and sweets. These gifts enabled us to help many older people (we sent out over two hundred parcels to them) and to send gifts into homes in this district.[110]

The definitive evidence was eventually provided by Revd Kenward's granddaughter Mrs Ann Sayer who had been looking through her father's many articles about Crossway and found several references to Queen Mary's visit. The Queen ordered the church magazine and obviously sent items to Crossway for people in need. She also sent a wall hanging with a quotation from Psalm 19: *'Let the words of my mouth and the mediation of my heart be acceptable in thy sight, O Lord.'* On the reverse, presumably in the Queen's hand, is written, *'For Mr and Mrs Kenward with best wishes from H.M. the Queen Christmas 1920 – Buckingham Palace.'*[111]

---

[110] *Crossway Chronicle,* February 1961, Crossway United Reformed Church archives.

[111] A photograph supplied by Revd Kenward's granddaughter Mrs Ann Sawyer.

In one undated article, Revd Kenward writes:

At that time (1917) the Palace phoned the office to say that Queen Mary had heard about the work that was being done at Crossway, and would visit that afternoon, so there was little time to do any spit and polish. Flo and Bert Kenward took their best tea set in order to entertain her Majesty in his vestry; the Queen duly arrived accompanied by Princess Mary and Lady Mary Trefusis her lady in waiting. They toured the building, and were greatly interested in the creche and signed the visitor's book. She was also very pleased to meet soldier and sailor's wives who met every afternoon for tea and knitted comforts for the men at the front. The party then went to the Minister's Vestry to take tea. Whilst this was being served 'in their best china', Queen Mary noticed a picture hanging on the wall of a bazaar that had recently been held. On studying this she noticed a man in the crowd and enquired who he was, as she had seen him when she entered the Church. Mr Kenward felt sure that the man in question was Mr Lipscombe, the superintendent of the Sunday School and a tailor by trade, who was not there. However, on the following Sunday he asked Mr Lipscombe if he had been at the spot where the Queen had noticed him. He said that he had almost hidden himself by the door that led to the creche and did not think anyone could possibly have noticed him, but it just goes to show how observant royalty are. After the tour the Queen asked for the Crossway magazine, a monthly paper, to be sent to her. This was done and for many years the Queen received this and on a number of occasions she sent articles that had been mentioned in the magazine for someone in need, in one case a twin pram. Some years later she read that Mr Kenward had had an operation and would be absent from the Church for some weeks; she immediately sent a great bunch of carnations from Sandringham and a get well card. Each year until Mr and Mrs Kenward retired they received a very large calendar at Christmas from the Queen.[112]

The Duchess of Gloucester

The Easter 1960 *Crossway Chronicle* reveals another royal connection to Crossway. The article explains that…

> *…for fifty or so years now Crossway has housed a kitchen of Invalid meals for London and worked easily with such a*

---

[112] Personal notes supplied by Mrs Ann Sawyer.

> *worthy voluntary effort. The London County Council is now taking over this service and the Duchess of Gloucester, president of Invalid meals visited us on 17th February 1960 to say good-bye to the staff. We found her so friendly and approachable, she talked to everyone in a quite unhurried and interested way. It is indicative of our times that such organisations are becoming obliged to ask to be taken over by local authorities but what a loss it is.*[113]

The Royal Family's interest in Elephant and Castle's churches has lasted a long time, perhaps due to its proximity to the palaces, and the people's clear need for support and encouragement.

Michael Caine

One of Elephant and Castle's most famous alumni is Sir Michael Caine (b. Maurice Micklewhite). In 2009 the locally-born actor made the film *Harry Brown* on the Heygate Estate using Crossway's Mayflower room as a 'Green Room' for the actors. During his promotion of the film, he told the *Evening Standard:*

---

[113] *Crossway Chronicle,* Easter 1960, Crossway United Reformed Church archives.

I come from this. I'm on these estates with these guys and they're talking to me like I'm one of them and I think, 'There but for the grace of God go I' ... The families have let the children down, the educators have let the children down. We've put them in rotten places like the Heygate estate ... which fortunately is being pulled down. It should never have been built.[114]

The image above is a photograph of a mural that adorned the front of Crossway's New Kent Road building, painted around 2006-08. In the middle is a depiction of the young Maurice Micklewhite as a child with his mother, having breakfast before going to school, and alongside it is an image of Michael Caine in the iconic film *Get Carter* (1971). During an interview at the Cannes Film Festival of 2010, Caine told a reporter that he had noticed the mural while filming *Harry Brown* and would like to own it if possible. News of this got to Revd Stevenson, who contacted the actor's people and in time arranged to take the artwork to his home in Leatherhead. On 30 April 2011 he loaded the three-panel work into his car and travelled with his wife and son to Surrey. On arrival Caine was rather curt and simply told the group to offload the items. His wife Shakira was more gracious and made out a cheque to cover the cost of the hire van.

---

[114] Louise Jury, 'Michael Caine: We've left children to rot, now they are animals', *Evening Standard,* 12 March 2009, accessed 29 April 2018, *https://www.standard.co.uk/news/michael-caine-weve-left-children-to-rot-now-they-are-animals-6827372.html.*

In a follow-up exchange of letters Caine agreed to become the church's patron, but was unable to attend the opening ceremony of the new building.

A dramatic location

Sir Michael Caine is not the only film star to have made a movie on the Heygate Estate. The Southwark Film Office was able to supply details of 25 licences granted between August 2010 and September 2011 for films, 'shorts', documentaries, fashion shoots and promotional videos that use the estate as a backdrop. They explained that while that was the total recorded on their current system, they were aware of other shoots that took place prior to the new database being installed.[115]

There are countless articles that document the extent of filming on the estate in the years leading up to its demolition, along with the reaction of the few local residents who remained there. Crossway benefitted financially by allowing many of the film crews to use the church's facilities. During Revd Stevenson's ministry they welcomed Clint Eastwood who was filming *Hereafter* (2010); although Matt Damon was the 'star' of the film, he was not required for the scenes that were shot on the estate and did not visit the area. The actor John Boyega, who went on to feature in *Star Wars: The Force Awakens* (2015), landed his first film role in *Attack the Block* (2011), which was filmed almost exclusively on the estate. The church was used extensively by the production company.

Television episodes of *Spooks, Ashes to Ashes* (starring Keeley Hawes and Philip Glenister), *Hustle, Silent Witness* and *The Bill* were also filmed on the estate, which became a premier location for any drama that needed a seedy-looking or run-down backdrop, usually to some violent or sinister plotline. It is little wonder, given the exposure that it received, that by 2012 the Heygate Estate was deemed to be a 'no-go area' by many people. Fewer than a dozen homes out of the 12,000 dwellings on the site were occupied by this time, and eventually the church became 'the last man standing' after Adrian Glasspool was forcibly evicted from his three-bedroom maisonette at lunchtime on Wednesday 6 November 2013. The 39-year-old teacher had to leave after years of fighting Southwark Council. He spearheaded a campaign to get fair compensation for

---

[115] The Southwark Film Office, email to the author, 22 February 2018.

leaseholders who were required to vacate their properties under compulsory purchase orders. *The Independent* newspaper ran several articles about his plight. One such piece that gives a good summary of events can be found on the publication's website.[116]

One of the nicest celebrities to use the church as a 'Green Room' was Bradley Walsh, who at the time was starring alongside Freema Agyeman and Jamie Bamber in the popular British drama series *Law & Order: UK*. Revd Stevenson played host to the production company in 2011 as they filmed on the estate, and during a break asked Mr Walsh whether he would be available to meet with students from Globe Academy where Revd Stevenson was chaplain. He agreed, and ten pupils studying drama at the time were given the opportunity of interviewing Mr Walsh. His responses were inspirational and extremely positive, encouraging the young people to dream big. Mr Walsh hosts the daily game show *The Chase* and is to play one of *Doctor Who*'s assistants in the 2018 incarnation of the series.

Perhaps the funniest thing to be filmed on the estate stars Harry Hill and Paul O'Grady and is entitled *The Bill for the Summer Wine* (2010). It brings together the conclusions of two series – *The Bill* and *Last of the Summer Wine* – in a spoof drama.[117] It is one of the very few comic pieces to be produced at the location; most of the others are gritty dramas representing the area as a grimy cesspit of social deprivation.

A more balanced view of the Elephant and Castle is provided in a short film presented by the journalist and author Michael Collins. It features the Heygate Estate, on which Collins grew up, and gives helpful background information as well as exploring the role it played in his life. It was first shown on BBC Four but can now be viewed on YouTube[118].

---

[116] Emily Dugan, 'End of an era for notorious Heygate estate: social housing gives way for high rise in prices', *Independent,* 8 November 2013, accessed 28 February 2018, *http://www.independent.co.uk/news/uk/home-news/end-of-an-area-for-notorious-heygate-estate-social-housing-gives-way-for-high-rise-in-prices-8929998.html.*

[117] Harry Hill and Paul O'Grady, *The Bill for the Summer Wine,* published on YouTube 31 December 2011, accessed 28 February 2018, *https://youtu.be/YudDIQx8ogo.*

[118] Michael Collins, *The Great Estate: The Rise and Fall of Social Housing,* August 2011, published on YouTube 6 November 2011, accessed 28 February 2018, *https://www.youtube.com/watch?v=WVGMyo40SyE.*

From princes to paupers, Crossway has served them all and continues to be a place of welcome and hospitality to anyone wishing to share the space.

CHAPTER SEVEN

For All the Saints

THERE ARE A GREAT MANY PEOPLE WHO MAKE UP CROSS-way and it would be a mammoth task to name everyone. It is the sum of all the people that results in a community of faith that collectively defines the church.

Chapter 4 has already featured the clergy. In this section we want to honour some of the other people who have played a significant role in building the church community. Their names are recorded in the archives and annuals, but their stories are largely forgotten except by those who worked closest with them.

The chronicler of Crossway: Ernest H. Jeffs

One such person was Ernest H. Jeffs, the author of the first ten annual reports of Crossway Central Mission Church. Born in Warwick in 1860, Jeffs moved to London and married Jane in 1909. Jeffs spent a decade describing the life, work and witness of the church – which was originally to be called the South London Mission, but was renamed following some confusion with the Methodist South London Mission in Bermondsey – in a series of booklets. His first was entitled, 'A Few Words ... Inauguration Day', in which he describes the service and the dignitaries that attended.[119] In 1910 he made 'The Case for Crossway' in which he urged the London Congregational Union to financially support work of

---

[119] Ernest H. Jeffs, 'A Few Words ... Inauguration Day', 1905, CH.A.6 (7), Dr Williams's Library, London.

Crossway in the Elephant and Castle.[120] A year later he captured the life of Crossway in his title, 'Snap Shots by Pen and Camera'.[121]

Ernest went on to produce *Princes of the Modern Pulpit: Religious Leaders of a Generation* in 1931, and *The Doctor Abroad: The Story of the Medical Missions of the London Missionary Society*[122]. He became editor of *The Christian World* in 1936. He died in 1973, at the age of 88.

Members of the congregation

In the archive that remains for Crossway is a Roll of Church Members from 1933 until around 1957. Its general remarks column provides a glimpse of the changing Crossway community and what became of its one-time members. Exact dates of admission are not recorded for everyone, but we do learn that Mr and Mrs Elkins – firstly of Burnell Street, Blackfriars Road, later moving to 206 Doddington Grove – were *'original members when [the] church formed'* on 3 December 1905, as was Miss Pays of Larcom Street. Deaths, departures and a few resignations are recorded. We learn of a Mrs Arnold who became a missionary, as did Mr Able, who is listed as being *'in India working under the L.M.S. [London Missionary Society]'*. Pencilled annotations provide updates on other members of the congregation, such as Mr Bagley, the former caretaker who moved to a London County Council rest centre and Miss Bolton, who joined Civil Defence.

The Roll of Church Members includes several poignant entries from the Second World War. Miss Emily Williams is reported as being part of the Auxiliary Territorial Service, which was the women's branch of the British Army during the conflict. It was formed on 9 September 1938, initially as a women's voluntary service, and existed until 1 February 1949 when it was merged with the Women's Royal Army Corps. While some members served, others were lost in the fighting. A Mrs Dunkley, we are told, was *'killed by [a] raid in 1940'*; Mrs Faultless is recorded as *'missing after [a] raid in 1940'*; and Mr Sloane was *'killed in [an] air raid'*.

The records were rewritten in October 1942 and designated as a 'Roll of Active Church Members'. Crossway membership statistics indicate

---

[120] Ernest H. Jeffs, 'The Case for Crossway', 1910, CH.A.6.(9), Dr Williams's Library, London.
[121] Ernest H. Jeffs, 'Snap Shots by Pen and Camera', 1911, CH.Lo.P.129, Dr Williams's Library, London.
[122] London: Livingstone Press, 1934.

that membership plummeted during this period from 173 in 1938 to 64 in 1947.[123] While this might be down to the impact of the war, the document also records some more personal tragedies from this period. Two members are recorded as being re-married at Crossway: Mr Adamsbaum is described as ex-Jewish and his bride, Mrs George Clarke, as ex-Roman Catholic. Sadly, Mr Adamsbaum's death is recorded just two years later. Another sad story behind the recorded detail must surely be that of Mr and Mrs Walter and Bessie Perrott. He died on 24 May 1945, and she died just three weeks later, on 15 June 1945. However devastating their loss must have been for the family, perhaps they could take solace that the love that united the two on earth became a marriage made in heaven.

Crossway's records were reconstituted again in 1952 but without the same level of detail. However, there is one person from this period who deserves a special mention.

Winnie's Story

Edith Winifred 'Winnie' Thomas of 37 Fleming Road is recorded as becoming an associate member in 1944. Associate membership in the Congregational Union is an unusual thing, suggesting a close affiliation with the church but without the rewards or responsibilities of full membership. But while there is no record of her becoming a full member, Winnie's relationship with Crossway was to last nearly 70 years until her death in 2013, and her contribution was sacrificial and total.

Miss Thomas's association with Crossway began during the Second World War, when she was required to 'volunteer' as a youth worker as part of the reparations required of her by a judge who found her guilty of being a conscientious objector. She had refused to sign up or work in a munitions factory as her Christian faith and pacifist beliefs made it impossible for her to accept work in these fields. God moves in mysterious ways, to use that famous misquotation of the Bible (that may allude to Romans 11:33 or Isaiah 55:8-9) coined in the hymn by William Cowper in 1773. The judge's requirement for Miss Thomas to work in a local church was an inspired decision, and Winnie's name appears

---

[123] Data recorded in the Congregational Handbook, Dr Williams's Library, London.

frequently in subsequent minutes and records, showing her to be a dedicated and loyal member of the church.

As a teenager Winnie formed a special friendship with Miss Kathleen Hutchings of 209 Hillingdon Street, and the two went to a Methodist church in the area. Kath was employed as a telephonist, which meant that she was not required to change her job for the war effort. She eventually joined Crossway in February 1952 and the two became inseparable, setting up home together at 13 Netherby Road, Forest Hill, on 16 November 1972.

One of Winnie's longest lasting contributions was as Captain of the Girls' Life Brigade. The modern organisation was formed by the amalgamation of three like-minded groups in 1964: the Girls' Brigade of Ireland (founded 1893), the Girls' Guildry of Scotland (1900) and the Girls' Life Brigade of England (1902). Because of its centrality to Winnie's life, it is worth exploring the history of the organisation in some depth. The website describes its founding ethos:

> In 1902, Girls' Life Brigade church mission groups began to emerge. GLB was spurred on by an English church initiative amongst children, 'the Sunday School movement'. However, GLB went beyond a focus on solely teaching the Bible, and moved beyond Sunday as the only key time in a week set aside by church for girls to discover how God fits in to their lives.

> Like GB of Ireland and Girls' Guildry, GLB met during the week, offering girls the opportunity to develop in their whole lives, based on the discovery of what it meant for God to love them and gift them in unique ways.

> This holistic mission engaged girls into all kinds of activity and opportunity, with God at the centre. Christian leadership and service were hallmarks of GLB, and girls were soon learning that, whatever their age, they have unique gifts, purpose and hope. Centred around discovering what it meant to be loved by God, and to love others in the same way, GLB aimed to help girls become responsible, self reliant Christian women.

> During the founding years of GLB's mission work the social, political and economic background of Britain was beginning to change for women. And as women began to gain a voice and a new place of contribution and influence in their world,

> *GB was making a Godly contribution to shaping the lives of many of these emerging women!*[124]

The original GLB badge was changed when the three constituent organisations combined. In the centre of the new version is a cross, the symbol of Christ and His church. Below it is a lamp, that His glory may shine out upon the world. Above it, a crown, that we may own Christ as our King. Behind it all, a torch, the flame of Christ's living spirit and our devotion to Him.

The GLB's guiding principles are to acknowledge Jesus Christ as Saviour and Lord according to the scriptures, and to fulfil its role to the glory of one God, Father, Son and Holy Spirit. The Brigade witnesses to the standard set by Jesus Christ and gives positive teaching on the Christian attitude to life. It promotes a just society where all people are equally valued. A Girls' Brigade member will do her best to be loyal to company and church, to be honest, truthful, kind and helpful; and to remember the Girls' Brigade motto: *'Seek, Serve and Follow Christ'*. Miss Thomas epitomised the aims of the Brigade, *'to help girls to become followers of the Lord Jesus Christ and through self control, reverence and a sense of responsibility to find true enrichment of life'*.[125]

---

[124] 'Story So Far', Girls' Brigade website, accessed 12 February 2018, *http://gbworldwide.org/about/story-so-far/*.
[125] *Ibid.*

Miss Thomas qualified as a teacher in 1960, taking up a position at Peckham Secondary School. Although a period of ill health restricted her contribution to Crossway, she remained dedicated to her faith and service to the church. Miss Thomas served Crossway in a number of different ways – organising social events, leading the GLB, representing Crossway and supporting members pastorally. In his inaugural newsletter Revd Boorman wrote:

I have realised how much Crossway is indebted to our now one and only full time worker other than myself, Miss Winifred Thomas. She has done and is doing a great job here.[126]

When he appointed her Church Secretary on 24 February 1963, her first act was to praise another, by mentioning Rita McCarthy's good work in church. This sort of encouragement and support for others was typical of Miss Thomas. By November 1963 Miss Thomas was chairing the Church Meeting in the absence of Revd Boorman who had resigned his post, and it was proposed that she lead the Christmas morning family service the following month.

By the early 1970s congregation numbers for Sunday worship had become woefully low, but the church's groups and organisations continued to thrive. During Easter 1972, Revd Ralph Essex wrote in a pastoral letter:

Today we are very small in numbers. If we get six Crossway members to a service we are doing well. At the same time the Girls' Brigade run by Miss Thomas and Miss Hutchings is flourishing.[127]

This was a time of great change for the church and the neighbourhood as many old buildings were demolished to make way for the new Heygate Estate. Writing in summer 1976 a district visitation team led by Revd D.J.D. Baker reports:

Membership looks ridiculously low in the year book, but is in fact optimistic. At this point, attempts to list Crossway along

---

[126] Stanley Boorman, *Crossway Chronicle,* April 1957, Crossway United Reformed Church archives.
[127] Ralph Essex, pastoral letter, Easter 1972, Crossway United Reformed Church archives.

with other United Reformed Churches breaks down. There are only three members young and fit enough to take an active part in the life of the Church (they do so by running Girls' Brigade and helping in Sunday School and Women's meetings).[128]

Although they are not named, two of the three are likely to be Miss Thomas and Miss Hutchings. The report indicates that by this point Miss Thomas was no longer secretary, as the minister's role is described as including the duties of warden of the building, secretary and assistant treasurer. In 1983 it was reported that Girls' Brigade had four sections and a total membership of 65.

Miss Thomas was also instrumental in starting a youth service at the church called Crossway Praise. As part of the AGM held on 29 April 1990 she remarked:

Although our numbers are not large we have often enjoyed joyful worship. The children's attendance has continued to be erratic but until recently a group of boys from Pilot and girls from G.B. as well as a number of little ones have attended regularly. This year has seen the beginning of bi-annual family services and G.B. / Pilot Parade services. Some have been quite well attended with a few parents accompanying their children. We hope that this participation will grow into a strengthening of our fellowship.[129]

Typically, Miss Thomas acknowledged and applauded the hard work of everyone else and encouraged them with her appreciation. While she was an ever-present member of the church meeting, the minutes suggest that Miss Thomas chose to keep her counsel. In the background she would help people and pour balm onto difficult situations.

Miss Thomas's long-time friend Kath died in February 2009, but Winnie continued to make the four-and-a-half-mile journey from home to church. Towards the end of her life she gave good advice and was

---

[128] URC Bromley District visitation report, Summer 1976, Crossway United Reformed Church archives.
[129] Church Meeting minutes, 29 April 1990, Crossway United Reformed Church archives.

always supportive, knowledgeable, kind and loving. She was certainly one of the saints that built Crossway.

All the saints

Naturally, there are many others worthy of mention: people such as the Girls' Brigade (GB) captains who followed Miss Thomas, and Barbara Caley who became a commissioner of the GB and continues to assist and support the 156th London group in the new building. She was followed in February 1998 by Maureen Jackson who also led Crosspatch, a mothers and toddlers group. She in turn was succeeded by her daughter Amanda (Mandy) Buckberry on 2 October 2011, assisted by her husband Russell.

The Purley Queens

Another group of people who have contributed to Crossway are the Purley Queens. These are not followers of the organised charitable tradition of London working-class culture known as pearlies, but a group of people who came from the suburbs and gave their time by visiting people in the neighbourhood. An early reference to the Purley Queens is found in the December 1959 edition of *Crossway Chronicle*. One of the entries gives thanks for the life of Mrs Gladys Crawford from Hayes Free Church, who died suddenly and whose place was taken by two ladies from Hayes. In September 1961 Revd Boorman writes:

> *We must place on record our deep and grateful thanks to our Church at Sanderstead for two years of help with our Sunday School, during which time and because of their help we have more than doubled our numbers. Some of their young men who have been helping us in this way are soon to give up and we will be seeking Sunday morning help particularly for teaching boys. When we receive help like this the result is always astonishing. We know that from the teams of visitors from Purley and Hayes who help us so loyally and effectively month after month.[130]*

---

[130] *Crossway Chronicle,* September 1961, Crossway United Reformed Church archives.

In the September 1965 newsletter, Revd Ashdown gives thanks to Miss Bessell who *'comes to us from Balham each Tuesday afternoon to play for our Women's meeting'*. She had done so for many years. Revd Ashdown also recognised the work of Mrs Lewis from Lewisham Church who, also on Tuesdays, looked after records and outings. Mrs C.W. Jones from West Wickham was commended for couriering *'half a dozen handicapped women to the meeting in her car'*. Mrs Jones visited 'shut-ins' (disabled church members who could not attend in person) on Tuesdays, and since her move to Tenterden it was wondered who might do this work. It is evident from these magazine snippets that Crossway was reliant on the help they received from the surrounding churches.[131]

Elizabeth Pye-Smith and Alison Morgan spoke about their involvement at Crossway during a meeting on 19 September 2017 with Revd Brian Pavett to talk about his time as minister. They were regular pastoral visitors and invited women to strawberry teas in Purley. Alison later emailed the author:

> *Since before the war Purley had a connection with Crossway. A number of ladies visited the housebound, took them for drives in the Surrey countryside and provided tea in their gardens. Several of us who were teachers helped with the holiday club run with the Anglicans in St Matthew's, probably in the 1970s. Somewhere about the same time a group from Crossway joined us for a discussion and we went up to Crossway. I remember visiting one of the flats in a high rise block. Later during Peter Mac's [Revd P. McIntosh's] time a group of children came for a day and we went up on Farthing Down for a picnic and back to the church for a meal. A group of older people came in the summer for an outing and also for a Christmas party.*[132]

The phrase 'Purley Queens' is found in Revd Pavett's newsletter of April 1971 in which he says:

> *...the ladies have particularly appreciated Christmas parties at Purley and at Crossway provided by the good folk of Purley Church; also the gifts in kind which have been sent from numerous churches. The shut-ins among them continue to be*

---

[131] *Ibid.*, September 1965, Crossway United Reformed Church archives.
[132] Alison Morgan, email to the author, 20 September 2017.

visited by that faithful band of ladies (known affectionately as the 'Purley Queens') who through a good many years have continued diligently this invaluable piece of service. The joint Sunday School is at present passing through a lean period, but here again we are indebted to Dr Archer and Mr John Mander of Sanderstead for their continuing help in staffing the children's work.[133]

Another of the saints who helped the church was John Mander of Sanderstead. He was a 14-year-old member of the Sunday School there and responded to the call to help run Sunday School at Crossway. He travelled with Dr Simon Archer every week to provide leadership on Sunday afternoons. He continued to do this for six years. In a telephone conversation conducted during research for this book, he told the story of a single mum with four children that he got to know. Every Christmas she would help Crossway deliver gifts to others despite having little herself. He said it taught him the importance of resilience and resourcefulness, living life despite its difficulties. It was a lesson he had never forgotten.

There is anecdotal evidence from many churches in the suburbs that Crossway was helped and encouraged by many other congregations too. This tradition of support appears to have started when Revd Kenward made financial appeals at the beginning of the Mission's life, and it continued through the decades as the church received offers of help from far and wide. This situation only came to an end in 2014, when harvest goods were declined and account auditing was taken 'out of house'.[134] The value of this outsider support cannot be quantified, but it has ensured the church's existence up until this day, when it is finally in a position to support itself.

The church administrators and today's community

Crossway is rightfully appreciative of the church administrators whose minute-taking has produced some of the current archive. Barbara Caley served in this position from 1992 to June 1998, when she moved

---

[133] *Crossway Chronicle*, April 1971, Crossway United Reformed Church archives.
[134] For many year Diana Campbell, a member of Orpington URC, audited Crossway accounts, but when she was no longer able to do so an accountancy company was employed to do the job.

on to take up a position as court usher at The Old Bailey. Barbara was succeeded by Allyson White from July 1998 to February 2000. Gill Webb became the administrator in March 2000 and served until July 2008, followed by Irene Gondwe from January 2009 until Lydia Kaddu-Busawga took over in May 2010. These people were often the first point of contact for tradespeople and the congregation alike, fulfilling the role of property manager and pastoral carer in equal measure. They would work alone for long periods and field the many questions and enquiries from a host of disparate quarters.

Inevitably, the names of many of the saints who have 'built' Crossway are lost or were never recorded. This book is an opportunity to take a snapshot of the leadership team of 2018 for posterity. Among them are the Elders Stephenie Robinson, Rachel St Clair, B.B. Cobbinah, Adelaide Owusu (Secretary), Emmanuel Osei-Somuah, Eric Gyamfi and Sally Skaife. The treasurer is Sujeong (Christal) Bratley and the property consultant is John Whelan. The membership of 32 includes people from Ghana, Nigeria, Korea, Ecuador, Canada, Poland, Ireland, England, Switzerland, Ivory Coast, Togo, Jamaica and Zimbabwe. It will be these people who continue to build the church in the new building as people come and go from the area.

CHAPTER EIGHT

The Crossway Love Stories

LOVE HAS BEEN FOUND AT CROSSWAY. THREE MINISTERS have met and married during their time there. Another developed a lifelong friendship of mutual support and affection. They did not want their stories to be told in these pages. In this chapter, however, Rene Baterip shares her love story of how she met Jim, who was at one time the caretaker of the old Crossway building.

Memories of Crossway
FROM RENE & JIM BATERIP

> In early 1953, Jim started his first job in the offices of Pearce Duffs, a custard factory in Spa Road, Bermondsey, having left John Harvard School at Christmas. A pupil at the school was in the Boys' Brigade at Crossway, and about this time some of the older boys were being conscripted for National Service and having to leave, so members were being asked to invite friends to join. Jim was invited, and because there would be an opportunity to play football he joined. He enjoyed learning to play the bugle and was in the band. Church attendance was an essential requirement and Jim's mother insisted that he kept the rules. Mr Tom Harrison was the Boys' Brigade Captain and highly respected by all the boys and their parents alike.

> Because Rene had been born out of wedlock she had been placed in Dr. Barnardo's so that her mother could 'work for the war effort', and from there had been evacuated, initially to Long Melford, Suffolk, and then to Wells, Somerset. After the war she was returned to Dr. Barnardo's where she was returned to her birth mother and step-father. After two years she was placed in care for eight years with foster parents in Bournemouth where she belonged to a Congregational

Church, and became a junior member on profession of faith. At 16 years of age she came out of the care system and returned to her birth mother, and was seeking a church to attend. After seeing an advertisement for Boys' Brigade outside Crossway, and being familiar with that organisation in Bournemouth, she went along the following Sunday morning. There were not many people in church and disappointingly no young people. Rene went along the following Sunday. Again, a disappointing morning, except for one young lady she thought to be about the same age, so introduced herself. The start of a lovely friendship with Barbara: it was very encouraging. Evidently during August the Sunday school and the organisations closed down for the month, but they would be back the following week, and she would be there.

First week in September, 1955, the church came alive. Members of both the Boys' Brigade and Girls' Brigade were there, and other adults who had not been there the previous two weeks. Revd Douglas Watt was preaching, and after the service he spoke to Rene about helping in the Sunday school which met in the afternoons. He also explained that he and his wife were joint pastors of Crossway. Barbara also helped in the Sunday school, and explained that if you attended the evening service you were permitted to go to the Youth Club which met upstairs. She also encouraged Rene to join the Girls' Brigade, even though 16 years was quite an old age to join. The captain was Miss Win Thomas and Lieutenant Miss Kath Hutchins – great stalwarts of Crossway Central Mission for many, many years.

During the Remembrance Day morning service, 1955, as was the tradition, three of the young buglers from the Boys' Brigade band played the Last Post and Long Reveille. One of them was Jim. Following the service Rene congratulated him and told him they had played well. His arrogant answer was 'Of course we did' – not a good start, not that she had the faintest idea that he would become her soulmate for life. As it was Rene's first year in London, she and Barbara had arranged to visit the Cenotaph in Whitehall that afternoon following

Sunday school, to see the wreaths that had been laid there that morning. As they came out of the building a group of the BB boys were walking past on their way to the cinema, as was their usual practice; they would arrive late to the evening service then go to the Youth Club. However, Barbara had her eye on one of them and so asked them all to come along. They declined, with the exception of Eddie (to Barbara's delight), and Jim who said he wouldn't mind coming. This was the beginning of our courtship.

Douglas and Margaret Watt worked tirelessly building up the church. The Ladies Sisterhood meeting attracted at least 200 women; the Youth Club was at least 50 strong; Boys' Brigade numbered 30 to 40; Girls' Brigade about the same; and Sunday School for primary age children included at least 30. Yet with all these, the church only attracted about 30 church members, and deacons seemed to serve for many years.

The building was huge, housing all the above organisations. The ladies met in the church one afternoon a week. On Sunday evening all the youth were invited to the club rooms; they sometimes had a deacon or church member to lead discussions, or they played snooker and table tennis. The Youth Club met on two other evenings; when records were played and dancing took place. The GB and BB each met more than one evening a week. The local Babies Clinic rented one of the halls two afternoons a week: young babies were weighed weekly and mothers were able to see the health visitor and buy orange juice, cod liver oil and powdered milk. The Oddfellows, a temperance society, rented a hall an evening each month for their meeting. The Meals on Wheels Service dinners were cooked at Crossway, and we believe it was the WVS [Women's Voluntary Service] who used to deliver them to local elderly residents, Monday to Friday each week. An L.C.C. day nursery was at the top (back) of the building and the flat roof was fenced around for their playground. At the top front were three residential flats, one for the minister, one for the youth leader and one for the caretaker of the building.

In 1956 Mr Tom Harrison the BB captain died. The new captain was Mr Bill Selby, the son of one of the deacons. He had been a boy in the Company [the Boys' Life Brigade], but left to do his National Service and had only been married a year or two. Revd Watts asked Jim and Rene to take over the Life Boys (the junior BB). Complete novices, they visited other Life Boys sections to see how a normal evening was run, and went on an initial training course at the national BB training centre Feldon Lodge, Hemel Hempstead. Mr and Mrs Watts were very encouraging, as was the new BB captain and his parents. So their early courting days were given over to the Life Boys and visiting every boy's home, ensuring that parents were aware that attending Sunday School was an essential condition of belonging.

Later that year Jim's father was admitted to hospital suffering from TB, and his youngest brother – then three years old – was admitted to a different hospital with the same illness. In 1956 his mother was diagnosed with cancer, so Jim and Rene assisted with hospital visiting. Back in the 1950s, terminal cancer sufferers were not admitted to hospital, and Jim's grandmother and aunties looked after his mother at home.

In January 1957, Jim's mother died leaving eight children ranging from four to 18 years of age. The youngest was still in hospital suffering from TB and the next three were placed in a children's home. Jim and the other three remained at home with an alcoholic father and things were very difficult. Often left to their own devices it was no surprise that two of them fell foul of the law and one was placed in a residential remand home. He had an accident there and was very badly burned and was moved to East Grinstead burns unit. It did seem that Rene and Jim's courting days revolved around Boys' Brigade, hospital visits and the cinema on Saturday evenings.

Rene's home life too was not easy. Revd Margaret Watt arranged for her to move in with an elderly lady who went to the Women's Own. After about three months her step-father left home and Rene went home to her mother. At this time Rene and Jim got engaged to be married, thinking it would be

*at least two years before they would be able to do so.
However, at the end of May 1957 Rene's step-father returned
home and her mother gave her one week's notice to move out.
Having to find somewhere else to live would be expensive, and
with Jim's home life being so difficult, they sought advice from
Mr and Mrs Watt, who they held in high regard. Douglas
Watt agreed to marry them the following Saturday if they
obtained the special licence which was required. Mr Bill Selby
agreed to give Rene away and his neighbour let them use his
car. The wedding breakfast was held in the youth Room
upstairs in Crossway for 11 guests, and Bill's wife Gladys
prepared a ham salad meal and made a wedding cake. Rene
was able to buy a ballerina-length white wedding gown and
Bill arranged for a Boys' Brigade guard of honour outside the
church.*

*All this had to be arranged in a week, as well as finding a
furnished bedsit in Brixton to start married life. Any regrets?
None whatsoever. There have been ups and downs, yes, but
these true soul-mates have just celebrated their Diamond
Wedding – 60 years.*

In a subsequent telephone conversation Rene spoke more about their
time at Crossway. The couple wanted to move into unfurnished
accommodation and the church was advertising for a caretaker. Jim was
successful and took up the position in the summer of 1958. He was paid
£6 per week, less national insurance. Within two months Rene became
pregnant with their first child. The relationship between the couple and
the new minister's wife, Mrs Boorman, was a little strained; after all, she
and Revd Boorman had four children and needed more space than Revds
Douglas and Margaret Watts had before them. In 1960 council-allocated
homes were difficult to secure, and because Jim and Rene were in tied
accommodation the situation was harder: they were not allowed to go on
the waiting list, and if they left the caretaking job it would be considered
that they had made themselves voluntarily homeless.

Jim was not able to get a day off, because when he was not rostered
to work he would nevertheless have to get up early to get the boilers
working. In an attempt to improve his job prospects, he applied to the
Guinness Trust in Fulham, as it offered more money and a flat. He was
offered the position and accordingly gave one month's notice to

Crossway on 22 July 1960. Unfortunately, he was then taken ill and admitted into hospital with an ulcer. The Guinness Trust Board could not keep the job open and the church would not let him take back his notice.

Fortunately, or perhaps providentially, the Guinness Trust did offer Rene a flat on the Old Kent Road with days to go before they would have faced homelessness, as their notice period ended on 17 August 1960. Rene then set about moving their furniture three quarters of a mile by pram, walking backwards and forwards until everything was transported. She then told Jim what had been going on, so when he came out of hospital the family was in their new home and Jim had to find employment!

While Rene continued to worship at Crossway, Jim felt unable to join the church given the lack of love he had been shown and the difficulties that the family experienced. A minute recorded on Sunday 30 October 1966 notes that Jim and Rene wanted their membership to be transferred to the Baptist Church at Harlow where Jim had become a Life Boy Leader. *'This was agreed by church members.'*[135]

It has been a privilege to tell one story of romance at Crossway – but this is probably just the tip of the iceberg. One wonders how many more there are?

---

[135] Rene Baterip, email to the author, 12 January 2018.

CHAPTER NINE

The Next Chapter

IN THIS LAST CHAPTER THE STORY OF CROSSWAY IS brought up to date (2018) with the church in the new building: Crossway Christian Centre, 18 Hampton Street, London, SE1 6SN. Practical completion was granted on 15 February 2017 and a number of opening events were held culminating in a Civic Service on 26 April. The people who were involved in the construction – who 'built' Crossway in the literal sense – must be recognised, and further information about the planning process and execution of the project can be found elsewhere in these pages.[136] This publication also recognises the membership as at the time of writing[137] and details of the user groups involved[138].

Much of the detail of the events leading up to the move can be traced through Revd Stevenson's annual reports, which were submitted to the URC General Assembly Special Category Ministry Group, Synod Area Pastoral Committee and Church Members. They plot the highs and lows of the project and indicate the determination, persistence and perseverance required to bring it to fruition.[139]

The last days of the Heygate Estate

In 2006 Southwark Council began to relocate the residents of the Heygate Estate of which Crossway was part. Before long, most of the residential properties were vacant and boarded up. There were 50, mainly leasehold, properties still occupied in 2009 and the last resident left in 2013, resulting in Crossway being the only inhabited building on

---

[136] See Appendix I – The People who Built Crossway.
[137] See Appendix II – Members of Crossway United Reformed Church.
[138] See Appendix III – User Groups at Crossway Christian Centres.
[139] Peter Stevenson, annual report, 2010, Crossway United Reformed Church archives.

the estate for the following four years. Throughout this period, the church was on the lookout for a place to move.

In February 2010 Revd Stevenson met with Kim Humphries, who was at the time a Conservative councillor and the Executive Member for Housing and Deputy Leader of Southwark Council. (He went on to become the community engagement lead for the developer Delancey.) Mr Humphries was encouraged to hear that five congregations met at Crossway and felt this was a better 'bargaining chip' than the 19 members of the church. He applauded the way in which the building was being used and urged the church to negotiate from this position of community involvement and engagement.

The political situation in the borough changed completely following the local election of 6 May 2010, when a shock result meant that the Liberal Democrat / Conservative coalition was replaced by majority Labour control. The new leadership wasted no time in getting a 'Heads of Terms' agreement with construction company Lendlease to develop the Heygate Estate, which was signed on 7 July 2010. The council agreed to provide Lendlease with vacant possession of the land which started the 'countdown' to when the church had to be off the estate. The agreement was that the land would be vacant by 21 September 2016.[140] That date seemed a long way off at the time, but it worked to the church's advantage as the date got closer.

By the end of 2011 initial hopes of moving into the redundant Walworth Town Hall had evaporated because the Synod considered it to be too big for the church to manage. They were concerned that the building would need dedicated full-time staff to manage the lets, and without someone taking responsibility the scheme would falter. At the time, the church did not have a leadership structure of Elders, neither was there a secretary or treasurer. The result was over-reliance on the Minister, who was supported by a part-time administrator and cleaner. The Town Hall would also require funding estimated at £3m in order to be redeveloped, and although £1.1m had been secured by the church, there was still a long way to go. The Synod withdrew their support, leaving Crossway without the necessary backing.

Meanwhile, life went on at the church itself. In the annual report from this period, Revd Stevenson reported that, outside of matters to do with

---

[140] This was the 'long-stop' date in the Heads of Terms agreement between the church and the council.

the building project, he was involved in chaplaincy to Globe Academy, a local secondary school, and Southwark Council's offices in Tooley Street. His report continues:

> *Attempts to run bible studies and midweek groups have largely been unsuccessful with just three or four members committed. BB Cobbinah recently started a Friday evening healing service that is attracting interest, but mainly from people outside the Crossway congregation. This is the third incarnation of this ministry and it is hoped that it will grow further. We held a joint harvest service with people remaining on the Heygate estate. Although the planning was difficult there was goodwill for the event from both communities. We were delighted with the joint carol service that brought together all the congregations using the building and hope this might be the start of further joint worship services.*[141]

A new site is found

On 18 May 2012 Southwark Council proposed a site in Hampton Street, suggesting that a new building could be designed on the footprint of the former Castle Day Centre. During negotiations, there was a breakdown in the relationship between the Synod and Southwark Council, and the situation was only narrowly saved by some timely intervention by the church to broker the negotiations. With the help of Charles Young, an artist and architectural student from Edinburgh who was working alongside Paul Sharrock of Thomas Ford and Partners, some initial designs were offered. These drawings, plus a clear vision statement from Crossway, were presented to the Synod moderator Nicola Furley-Smith on 31 May 2012. Approval was given, and the focus adjusted to delivering the best possible replacement for the existing church building.

As work to replace the Crossway building progressed, Revd Stevenson clearly found the role of building the church challenging, as his report at the end of 2012 reflects:

> *I often consider what the purpose of Crossway United Reformed Church is and have been asking myself, 'Why would*

---

[141] Peter Stevenson, annual report, 2011, Crossway United Reformed Church archives.

God allow and enable Crossway to remain in the Elephant and Castle in 2013?'

Our ministry to children and young people is poor. Beyond the work of a few involved in GB and the Sunday Groups we offer little in the way of discipleship, nurture or encouragement.

Our outreach is limited, our pastoral care for each other is patchy, our spiritual development lacks commitment and our numerical growth is negative. Financially the church survives on the business it can generate and we have only recently managed to introduce a leadership team. An outsider might justifiably ask, 'Why do you continue?'

How would you answer that question? It is a question that the Synod has asked, as well as the council negotiators and a few of my colleagues.

The Special Category Ministry task at Crossway remains: build a church; build a congregation and build a community. The first is progressing and it is hoped that URC Southern Synod Trust Co will soon sign a Heads-of-Terms agreement with Southwark Borough Council to enable work to start on preparing the ground for a new church building 350 meters from our current position. The last element of the task is also progressing well and Crossway is well known in the area and increasingly used and approached by the community. The middle part of the task takes us back to the original question, 'What is the purpose of Crossway?'[142]

At the beginning of January 2013, the URC Synod Trust Co and London Borough of Southwark agreed on a 'Heads of Terms' document in order to procure a new building in Hampton Street. Another six months passed before Mott MacDonald was eventually appointed to lead the design team with Josh McCosh and David Soro of van Heyningen and Haward as the project architects. Their appointment on 28 June 2013 resulted in a flurry of activity. By the end of the year the project had reached RIBA C (feasibility study), with a preplanning application

---

[142] Peter Stevenson, annual report, 2012, Crossway United Reformed Church archives.

submitted and an invitation extended to Geoffrey Osborne (Builders) to tender for the work. Up to this point the project had benefitted greatly from the support of Paul Sharrock and Simon McCormack of Thomas Ford and Partners, who advised the URC and submitted the early plans and block drawings.

In the meantime, the existing Crossway building required maintenance and care. It had been trespassed on six occasions in one year, with varying degrees of damage and cost. The unwanted attention also concerned the insurers who put additional requirements on the church in order to retain cover. In his end of year report for 2013, Revd Stevenson writes:

> *As I approach the end of my first five years at Crossway I would mark myself 7/10 for building a church, 8/10 for building a community and 5/10 for building a congregation. There is still much to do and the challenges are often seemingly too much to bear but by God's Grace and to His glory all will be well and all will be well.*[143]

By the end of the following year, his pessimism had worsened:

> *...the congregation has shrunk further; the neighbouring properties have been demolished; the minister is less involved in the community; most of the work has been about property.*[144]

There was a delay to proceedings at the end of July 2014 when the new building scheme was halted by London Borough of Southwark. The design, which had been worked on for the previous 15 months, was declared over-budget and the council felt unable to justify the costs. For a while it was unclear what would happen, but the design team reformed and started working on a smaller, cheaper option for the site. The alternative did not reduce the specification for the church but stripped out the planned residential element. By the end of the year the scheme was back on track and a planning application had been lodged.

---

[143] Peter Stevenson, annual report, 2013, Crossway United Reformed Church archives.
[144] Peter Stevenson, annual report, 2014, Crossway United Reformed Church archives.

It was already known that the neighbours on the adjacent Draper estate were against the development, in part because it took away resident parking in the garages that were below the original building. In a *Southwark News* article of 16 October 2014 the reporter Amelia Burr writes:

> *A housing estate plagued by one problem after another is now losing its garages to make way for a new 'multiplex' church. On Saturday Draper residents will lose their precious garages, which are to be knocked down to make way for the Crossway United Reformed Church, after it was made homeless by the Heygate regeneration.*[145]

They were also concerned about the number of vulnerable people that would be brought onto the estate because the church catered for people in need. Meetings with the Tenant and Resident Association took place throughout the process and resulted in a number of major design changes.

At the same time there were tensions within the development team as Southwark Council began to reflect on the costs of the development. The council urged the project managers to value engineer the project, forcing the developer to reduce quality, which was not acceptable to the URC. During 2014 there were a number of exchanges of views, but the church held onto the existing 'Heads of Terms' agreement and as the deadline for Crossway to vacate its Heygate home got closer, the negotiations intensified. In the end the church got most of what it wanted, and full planning permission was granted on 3 March 2015.[146]

On 6 August 2015, in a personal diary entry, Revd Stevenson records:

> *The wheels have fallen off again!! After the planning application was successful it was thought that we might be in a position to get the building works started but Osborne's cost plan analysis, Mott McDonald's value for money advice and London Borough of Southwark's budget could not come together...*
>
> *In the meantime Synod Trust is wobbling – another church (Richmond Green) is closing within ten years of a redevelop-*

---

[145] Amelia Burr, writing in *Southwark News,* 16 October 2014.
[146] Southwark Council planning department archives.

ment and the trust are liable for a large VAT bill as a result. This has got the Synod Trust anxious and the officer has been instructed to find out what would happen if we pulled out of the Development Agreement.

Mood and humour up and down but health good after being on the 2/5 diet since February and losing a stone and a half in weight.

However, by the end of the year and after a great many meetings and further negotiations, the build was back on track. Revd Stevenson's end of year report makes for happier reading:

It is good to report positively at the end of this year. After six years in post and after a few failed attempts to get a scheme approved, ground on the new church building has been broken! It has taken since 18th March 2012, when London Borough of Southwark offered the site which the church is being built on, to get an acceptable design, develop the planning application and achieve all the financial packages. Work started on 16th November 2015 and is due to be completed by 5th December 2016.

The Development Agreement requires the council to provide Crossway with a suitable church that satisfies modern building and legal requirements. The church has requested that the new building achieves the best performance possible with the least maintenance requirements. The architects feel that the design has achieved this and the developers are keen to illustrate the quality of the build and the materials being used. In addition to the church building, the agreement provides for residential property either in the form of a three-bed freehold house or two flats (the flats were never built due to costs). Together with another property under the control of Crossway the longer-term financial position of the congregation has been secured. It will be able to contribute to the wider church while at the same time having choice regarding how it organises its mission and outreach programmes.

The Eldership that was formed in 2014 has begun to recognise their leadership role and have agreed, as a group, to attend Embracing Eldership training at Westminster College in Cambridge next year. They have met the building users group and started to take decisions about how the new building is to be operated. During the summer we worked on a mission statement and developed operational processes. The documents included a Building Management paper, new letting agreements, and a charter of missional intent. The latter is an agreement that commits all the eight congregations of the current building to agree to mission together.

Sunday worship has developed over the past twelve months and there is greater support and commitment to fellowship together.

I took a conscious decision in September 2014 to stop many tasks in order to concentrate on a few key areas of ministry. The result was more time to reflect on the activities and outreach of Crossway and develop intentional mission. Lendlease, the developer of the site where the current church is located, approached me in the summer to offer a chaplaincy service. It was decided to accept their invitation on a one-year trial basis in order to closely link the church with the company. The work of establishing Crossway as a valued member of the community has largely been achieved and they regularly receive press coverage, support and encouragement.

While it has taken much longer than expected, the hard work, persistence and perseverance have begun to produce reward. It is satisfying to report positively in all three areas in the purpose of this Special Category Ministry and I look forward to the coming year and seeing the church building develop and all the dreams, visions coming to fruition.[147]

For Revd Stevenson, much of 2016 was filled with donning five-point PPE (Personal Protective Equipment) for the chaplaincy on the Lendlease Elephant Park site and the church's own building development. As work

[147] Peter Stevenson, annual report, 2015, Crossway United Reformed Church archives.

progressed, the site managers Mike Saxton, Neal Mansukh and later Nathan Cocks were supportive and gracious, always explaining the progress and at times lack of it. Experts in various different trades were on site for long periods: among them were Dean Choules and Harry Marsh of Laser Electrical; Danny Harrington of ACP (Air Conditioning Projects); and carpenter Mark Wale. In total, over 500 people were involved and many positive, if temporary, relationships were formed. There was a very enjoyable Christmas outing in the local hostelry that year.

The end of year report in 2016 reflected on the progress that had been made, and the challenges remaining:

> *The only thing now missing is a solid congregation that regularly meets for worship and acts as a fellowship. There is a core of 10 to 15 [people] that carry the responsibilities of the church and we are indebted to members like Mandy and Russell Buckberry for their constant and loving leadership of Girls' Brigade; to BB Cobbinah for her healing ministry and leadership of Friday Night Prayers; the Eldership and treasurer for their growing confidence; the employed staff, Lydia and Zeno for their care and consideration of the finance and fabric of the building; the worship team of Mandy, Christal Bratley and Stephenie Robinson for their ministry on Sunday mornings; and Ian who has been guiding our marketing strategy. I am grateful to Martin Hayward who acts as my line manager and helps me to reflect critically on the actions I take on behalf of the church. I believe that Crossway is in a great place and ready for evangelism and growth within the fellowship.[148]*

Crossway's Heygate Estate building was closed on 31 December 2016. After a couple of missed completion dates, partial completion made it possible for the new building to open on 15 February 2017. For six weeks, therefore, Crossway was without a home, but its members and leaders used this period as an opportunity to visit other churches locally and share worship and fellowship with them. Although it was hoped that all user groups from the old building would transfer to the new, in the

---

[148] Peter Stevenson, annual report, 2016, Crossway United Reformed Church archives.

event two organisations – a church and an asylum seekers' group – did not come.

Four opening events were planned, but in the end the users' service did not take place because of the delayed handover of the building. The first event for Crossway members actually took place on 15 January 2017, ahead of practical completion of the building, amid the dust and mess of the building site. The second opening event was for Synod on 25 March 2017. It was on this day that the moderator cut a cake and declared the building officially to be open. All the churches in the Synod were invited, but few attended. The main opening event was arranged for 26 April 2017. Sir Michael Caine originally agreed to attend but later withdrew his acceptance. Nevertheless a number of church and community personnel were present including the newly installed Bishop of Woolwich, Revd Dr Dorgu Karowei; the General Secretary of URC, Revd John Proctor; the General Secretary of Churches Together in England, Revd Dr David Cornick; the Mayor of Southwark, Cllr Kath Whittam; the former MP of Bermondsey and Old Southwark, Sir Simon Hughes; the CEO of Geoffrey Osborne, Andrew Osborne; Head of Regeneration at Southwark Council, Steve Platts; and the CEO of Edwards Insurance, David Edwards. Catering was supplied by Mamuśka Polish kitchen and bar, and music was performed by Valerie Malcolm, one-time lead singer of Groove Armada. Presentations were made by Josh McCosh of van Heyningen and Haward Architects, Paul Newell of Geoffrey Osborne, and Revd Stevenson.

A new chapter

At the time of writing in early 2018, Crossway is home to ten congregations, three day centres, and numerous community groups resulting in 65 per cent usage of the new building. The most significant growth seen in 2017 was the increase in the numbers attending Sunday morning and Friday evening worship. 40 new people attended the Sunday morning service that year, and 30 returned more than once, with 13 adults being accepted into church membership in February 2018. It was also pleasing to reintroduce the Sunday School in September 2017, as the numbers of children and young people coming to worship increased.

Crossway's new building has been widely praised. It was highly commended for the National Church Trust Presidents' Award (new church buildings category) in 2017 and was shortlisted for the prestigious

Royal Institution of Chartered Surveyors (RICS) community-use buildings award, the results of which were yet to be announced at the time of publication. Crossway has also been featured by Yamaha as an example of bringing people together.[149] On 16 July 2017 Professor Elna Solvang of Concordia College, Moorhead, Minnesota USA, contacted Revd Stevenson after a visit to the church by her students. She thanked him for introducing the students to the Elephant and Castle, and went on to say:

> *There are few congregations and few ministers with the vision and the stomach to persist through the years of uncertainty, obstacles, membership losses, and invisible 'progress'. I hope you write about this transformation so the narrative of the vision continues and so that other congregations and ministers might dare to do the same. I can think of a few congregations in my own Lutheran context who would resonate with the vision and the reorienting of congregational ministry towards the wider community (including my own little congregation in Fargo, North Dakota)...*
>
> *Students also connected your motivation, i.e. 'Because Jesus did it, I do it', to a challenge they had heard from Pastor Alan Storey (Central Methodist Mission, Cape Town) early on in the journey. Storey told the students that Jesus wasn't 'obsessed with you being obsessed with him' but that they should be 'committed to what Jesus was doing'. They also picked up on your commitment to finding solutions to social problems.[150]*

This book brings the story of Crossway up to date (for the time being). But it is never finished. There is still much more to do and say, and it is pleasing that there is a new purpose-built base from which to work. Is this the church that God built? Yes, but the church is so much more than bricks and mortar. Perhaps it should be concluded that, *this is the church that God is building!* AMEN.

---

[149] 'Crossway Christian Centre Brings People Together With Yamaha', Yamaha Pro Audio, October 2017, accessed 01 March 2018, *http://www.yamahaproaudio.com/europe/en_gb/news_events/newsrelease/2 017/1023_20_crossway.jsp.*

[150] Prof. Elna Solvang, email to the author, 16 July 2017.

APPENDIX I

The People who Built Crossway

Surname	First name	Company	Trade
Ababii	Victor	S R McHugh	Forklift Driver
Abbott	Jon	LB of Southwark	Regeneration
Adamovicius	Renatas	Trott	Ceiling fixer
Adams	Joe	Heritage Brickwork	Labourer
Amariutei	Adelino	CPS Cleaning Ltd	Cleaning
Anderca	Petre	Corbyn	Carpenter
Andrulis	Paulius	Madigan Gill	Plant operator
Anghel	Andrei	Corbyn	Carpenter
Aolarctei	I	Corbyn	
Arroyo Claudio	Luis	Corbyn	Crane operator
Ascott	G	A & K Services	Pipe fitter
Atkins	J	Van Elle	Test engineer
Aurania	A	Corbyn	Carpenter
Austin	David	Access Solutions	Scaffolder
Avis	Ivan	Corbyn	Groundworker
Aylett	Nick	King Lifting	Crane operator
Bafia	Marcin	TRT	Installer
Baker	Dan	MWC Roofing	Labourer
Baltag	V	MWC Roofing	Roofer
Barker	Trevor	Osborne	Contracts Manager

Surname	First name	Company	Trade
Bath	Karan	Corbyn	Concrete Finisher
Baxter	William	Dorabridge	Fabrication Welder
Baxter	Tony	Dorabridge	Steel Fixer
Bayly	Scott	MWC Roofing	Roofer
Beadle	Mark	S R McHugh	Labourer
Bennet	Scott	Van Elle	Steel Fixer
Bent	Jordan	Heritage Brickwork	Labourer
Bertie	Nycki	Osborne	Document Controller
Bewick	Neil	Simion Risk	H&S Advisor
Bieniek	Henryk	Trott	Plasterer
Biggs	Richard	FST	Fire Protection
Bird	B	London Tower Crane	Crane Erector
Blaga	Alia	CPS Cleaning Ltd	Cleaning
Blake	Dennis	Heritage Brickwork	Labourer
Blake	Danny	Access Solutions	Scaffolder
Blanco	Andrea	Heritage Brickwork	Labourer
Blyth	Paul	WFP	Alarm engineer
Bogdevic	Gzegoz	Trott	Fixer
Bogdevic	Anozei	Trott	Fixer
Bola	Tal	Ecolutions	Solar Electrician
Bonner	Tom	Shire	Carpenter
Brahimi	Elios	Corbyn	Pipelayer
Breckon-Payne	David	AC Projects	Ductwork fitter
Brodeala	Diana	CPS Cleaning Ltd	Cleaning

Surname	First name	Company	Trade
Brown	Billy	Access Solutions	Scaffolder
Brown	M	AC Projects	Director
Brown	Ray	Propak	Fixer
Brzozowski	Marcin	TRT	Installer
Budan	Michal	IMB Diamond Drilling Ltd	Driller
Budan	Nicolae	IMB Diamond Drilling Ltd	Driller
Buga	Vasile	Corbyn	Striker
Buju	Alex	Corbyn	Groundworker
Burbridge	S	CRA	AV Engineer
Burdfield	Michael	Access Solutions	Scaffolder
Burke	Martin	Heritage Brickwork	Bricklayer
Buttigieg	Emmanuel	Access Solutions	Scaffolder
Byatt	Chris	Ecolutions	Solar Electrician
Calane	Lonel	Corbyn	Labourer
Campbell-Smith	M	Optima	Tower Crane Op
Cantau	Stelian	Corbyn	o.m.
Carolan	Joel	Corbyn	Crane Supervisor
Cebotari	Vladimir	SRM	Labourer
Cendron	Andrea	Mott MacDonald	Project Manager
Chamberlain	J	Access Solutions	Scaffolder
Chamberlain	J	Access Solutions	Scaffolder
Chapple	Paul	Propak	Fitter
Chelaru	Uchard	EWS	Window fixer
Choules	Dean	Laser Electrical	Electrician
Christopher	Phil	TGA	Principle Design Man.
Ciubotaru	Ciprian	S R McHugh	Labourer

Surname	First name	Company	Trade
Clark	Mat	Mott MacDonald	QS
Clatworthy	Ron	AC Projects	Lagger
Coada	Durnitrui	Trott	Plasterer
Coe	Lloyd	MWC Roofing	Roofer
Coke	Nick	Mott MacDonald	Project Manager
Condon	Noel	NHE	Carpenter
Condranschi	Dorin	Corbyn	Steel Fixer
Conoscente	Doviole	Corbyn	Groundworker
Constantinsu	David	AC Beck & Sons	Painter
Cooney	Carl	Heritage Brickwork	Bricklayer
Cooper	Phil	AC Projects	Engineer
Cooper	D		Visitor
Corcoran	Stephen	Corbyn	Crane Supervisor
Cornish	Micky	Heritage Brickwork	Supervisor
Costea	Mihai	Corbyn	Carpenter
Costich	Dohel	Trott	Plasterer
Coulstock	Mick	Heritage Brickwork	Bricklayer
Cox	James	Pudlo	Site Support
Craig	Louis	Corbyn	Concrete pump op
Cross-Gower	M	Van Elle	Piling Foreman
Crowhurst	John	NHE	Carpenter
Crozier		London Tower Crane	Crane engineer
Cuckow	Sean	Access Solutions	Scaffolder
Cunningham	Shane	LB of Southwark	Accountant
Cunningham	Joe	MWC Roofing	Roofer

Surname	First name	Company	Trade
Cunnings	Daniel	Cunnings	Sound Technician
Cunnington	P	London Tower Crane	Crane Erector
Cunnington	S	London Tower Crane	Crane Erector
Davy	Richard	LendLease	Visitor
Daynton	Stuart	Mott MacDonald	Project Manager
Deacon	David	AC Projects	Lagger
Dean	Jonathan	Southern Synod URC	Surveyor
Delia	Nicolo	Heritage Brickwork	Labourer
Demian	Andrei		
Dermott	Leb	Van Elle	Engineer
Deruishi	Simon	Trott	Plasterer
Dilliway	Leyton	Braileys	Lightning Protection
Dilworth	Charlie	Dorabridge	Labourer
Djelpaoui	Smail	S R McHugh	Traffic marshall
Donnelly	N	Access Solutions	Scaffolder
Donovan	Ryan	Access Solutions	Scaffolder
Dorin	Badea	S R McHugh	Labourer
Dowling	Roy	AC Projects	Mech and Eng
Draga	Vlillnet	Trott	Plasterer
Dragoi	Iuliana	CPS Cleaning Ltd	Cleaning
Drazewski	Lukasz	London Wall	Installer
Dunne	Anthony	Heritage Brickwork	Bricklayer
Dziekan	Tomasz	Dorabridge	Steel Fixer
El-Gendy	Karim	London Wall	Fitter
Everest	Jay	Ecolutions	Solar Electrician

Surname	First name	Company	Trade
Exall	Matthew	Access Solutions	Scaffolder
Eyre	Natasha	Mott MacDonald	Mech and Eng
Fall	Assane	London Tower Crane	Crane Erector
Farmer	Matthew	AC Projects	Flue Fitter
Farrow	Paul	AC Beck & Sons	Paint Supervisor
Fawcett	James	Graf UK	Engineer
Fenwick	Dave	First Line Defence	Technician
Ferariu	C	Corbyn	Carpenter
Firth	Dean	Graf UK	Attenuation
Flanagan	Paul	NHE	Joiner
Fletcher	Malcolm	Floorcraft	Floorlayer
Fletcher	C		Visitor
Fletcher	Camilla	Ramboll	Acoustician
Focsa	Dmitri	MWC Roofing	Roofer
Foley	Michael	Access Solutions	Scaffolder
Forder	Scott	O'Neil Brennan	Crane Supervisor
Foster	M	London Tower Crane	Tower Crane Op
Frunza	Lucretia	CPS Cleaning Ltd	Cleaning
Funnell	Daniel	Access Solutions	Scaffolder
Furnadzhiev	Mihail	Trott	Fixer
Galea	Darren	AC Beck & Sons	Paint Supervisor
Gallagher	S	Floorcraft	Floorlayer
Galleal	John	TUV	Engineer Surveyor
Garayev	Chary	AC Projects	Plumber
Gardener	D	HAG	Door Systems
Garrett	Simon	Access Solutions	Scaffolder
Gibson	S	CP Electronics	Engineer

Surname	First name	Company	Trade
Gilmortin	Leon	AC Beck & Sons	Painter
Girjoaba	Ilie	Corbyn	Groundworks
Gladwin	Alex	A & K Services	Plumber
Golban	Alexander	Trott	Plasterer
Golban	Pavel	Trott	Plasterer
Graves	Jordan	Prodeck	Labourer
Green	Brice	AC Projects	Electrician
Greenan	Tom	London Tower Crane	Tower Crane Op
Gregson	Ric	NHE	Joiner
Grey	Daniel	First Line Defence	Engineer
Gurr	Peter		Engineer
Guy	Liam	Magicman	Magicman
Hadaway	Liam	Magicman	Magicman
Halili	Edison	Trott	Plasterer
Hamden	Hans	Sorba	Engineer
Hammerton	Wayne	FST	Painter
Hammond	David	Propak	Fixer
Hanson	Peter	van Heyningen and Haward	Architect
Hardie	Ian	Corbyn	Drain CCTV
Hards	Stephen	Access Solutions	Scaffolder
Harrington	Roger	AC Projects	Plumber
Harrington	Danny	AC Projects	Foreman plumber
Harrington	Paul	AC Projects	Plumber
Harris	Dwayne	AC Projects	Ductwork fitter
Harrison	Alex	AC Projects	BMS Installer
Healing	Richard	Shire	Carpenter
Healy	Simon	Propak	Fixer
Hemings	Tom	Corbyn	Apprentice

Surname	First name	Company	Trade
Henderson	S	Dorabridge	Fabrication Welder
Holdcroft	Joe	AC Projects	Electrician
Holt	Russell	AC Projects	Lagger
Holt	Lewis	AC Projects	Lagger
Horrigan	George	Access Solutions	Labourer
Hovsepyan	Vahe	MWC Roofing	Roofer
Humphreys	Peter	Cunnings	Sound Technician
Humphries	Steve	Prodeck	Manager
Hutchinson	Thomas	Ecolutions	PV engineer
Hutton	Warren	Propak	Fixer
Hyde	P	Corbyn	
Iacoban	Ghe	Corbyn	Carpenter
Isaacs	Nigel	AC Beck & Sons	Painter
Isufi	Z	Corbyn	Groundworker
Jackson	Daniel	Ecolutions	PV engineer
James	Alan	Floorcraft	Floorlayer
James	A		Visitor
Jefferson	Steve	Richardson roofing	Tinsmith
Jefferson	D	Richardson roofing	Tinsmith
Jefferson	Chris	Richardson roofing	Tinsmith
Jeffery	Carl	Heritage Brickwork	Labourer
Jenkins	Andrew	Access Solutions	Scaffolder
Johnson	B	AC Projects	Ductwork fitter
Johnson	Ian	Laser Electrical	Engineer
Johnson	Joe	Britelec	Data Engineer
Johnson	Lee	Laser Electrical	Data Engineer

Surname	First name	Company	Trade
Jukes	Joseph	Heritage Brickwork	Labourer
Kamara	Jermaine	Corbyn	Crane Supervisor
Kapitao-Paulo	Mario	AC Beck & Sons	Painter
Karabolli	Trifon	AC Beck & Sons	Painter
Karpinsk	Lukasz	Houton Construction Services	Carpenter
Kemp	Ashley	Access Solutions	Yard Manager
Kempster	Ashley	Access Solutions	Scaffolder
Kennedy	Gary	AC Projects	Engineer
Kettley	Jon	D & R	Steel erector
Kimmings	Steve	Speedy	Trim Engineer
Kinchev	Vasil	Trott	Fixer
King	Robert	Propak	Glazing
Kitson	Daniel		Visitor
Kota	Piro	Corbyn	Fixer
Kovaci	Dashamr	Corbyn	Labourer
Kucinskas	Judzas	Corbyn	Steel Fixer
Lander	Paul	WFP	Engineer
Lang	Andrew	First Line Defence	Supervisor
Lapkov	Georgi	Trott	Fixer
Larcombe	Matthew	ANCS	Crane engineer
Laukkanen	Perttu	Ramboll	Acoustician
Lawlor	D	Van Elle	Piler
Lawrence	Peter	AC Projects	Project Manager
Lee	Zachary	Guideline	Lift engineer
Lelliott	Ashley	First Line Defence	Plant operator
Lenghel	Dorina	CPS Cleaning Ltd	Cleaning

Surname	First name	Company	Trade
Leslie	Martin	Guideline	Lift installer
Lewis	Gary	AC Projects	Engineer
Light	Paul	NHE	Carpenter
Lindsay	George	Access Solutions	Labourer
Lindsay	Shaun	Access Solutions	Scaffolder
Lindsay	Tommy	Access Solutions	Scaffolder
Living	R	London Tower Crane	Supervisor
Loko	Silas	Heritage Brickwork	Labourer
Lovelock	Martin	A & K Services	Pipe fitter
Lozinski	Bartek	Corbyn	Machine driver
Lucescu	Daniel	Corbyn	Striker
Lunca	Danut	AC Beck & Sons	Painter
Lunca	Marian	AC Beck & Sons	Painter
MacDonald	Ken	Heritage Brickwork	Bricklayer
Macpherson	Paul	D & R	Steel erector
Macrai	Gheorghe	Corbyn	Labourer
Maier	Mariusz	Trott	Fixer
Manga	Umaro	S R McHugh	Labourer
Mansfield	Ian	Mott MacDonald	
Mansukh	Neal	Osborne	Site Manager
Manuela	Veronica	CPS Cleaning Ltd	Cleaning
Marsden	T	Access Solutions	Scaffolder
Marsh	Harry	Laser Electrical	Electrician
Marsh	M		Visitor
McArthur	Billy	AC Beck & Sons	Painter
McCauley	Liam	Van Elle	Piler
McCorkindale	Paul	CP Electronics	Engineer

Surname	First name	Company	Trade
McCormack	Simon	Thomas Ford & Partners	Surveyor
McCosh	Josh	van Heyningen and Haward	Architect
McGown	Alex	Van Elle	Steel Fixer
McGreal	Patrick	LB of Southwark	Surveyor
McHattie	Charlie	Ecolutions	Solar Electrician
McNeela	Daniel	AC Projects	Electrician
Medulics	Oleh	ESL	Landscaping
Michell	A	A & K Services	Plumber
Mihailica	Constantin	Corbyn	Carpenter
Mihali	Bogdan	EWS	Supervisor
Millard	Damon	AC Projects	Electrician
Mills	A	Openreach	BT Engineer
Mireniuc	Daniel	Corbyn	Steel Fixer
Moghrabi	Daniele	Rossoguil	Tape & Jointing
Monfries	Denver	BT Telecoms	Installer
Morfett	Guy	Southern Synod URC	Property Officer
Mulkerrins	Paraic	Corbyn	Groundworker
Mullings	Lewis	Heritage Brickwork	Labourer
Munday	Melvin	Dorabridge	Fabrication Welder
Murati	Eduart	Corbyn	Groundworker
Murbiru	Kenneth	Corbyn	Engineer
Murphy	Mykel	Access Solutions	Scaffolder
Murray	Stephen	Baker Dougan	Supervisor
Nash	Christopher	AC Projects	Flue Fitter
Nash	D	HAG	Door Systems
Necchi	P	MWC Roofing	Bitumen Roofer
Nelson	Kurt	Propak	Fixer

Surname	First name	Company	Trade
Newell	Paul	Osborne	Contracts Manager
Newton	Nick	Trott	Contracts Manager
Nica	Alin	Trott	Labourer
Nicholas	Brian	ARC Controls	Engineer
Norman	Ian	London Wall	Fitter
Nunn	J	CPS Cleaning Ltd	Air tester
Nusi	Edmondo	Corbyn	Groundworker
Nutt	Luke	Ecolutions	Solar Electrician
Nzekwe	Jude	Corbyn	Crane Supervisor
O'Brien	M	AC Projects	Lagger
O'Brien	William	Corbyn	Drain CCTV
O'Halloran	Phil	Corbyn	Crane Supervisor
Odere	Lawson	Optimum	Engineer
Okonkwo	F	SRM	Labourer
Olafare	Bunmi	LB of Southwark	Surveyor
Oliver	Simon	Van Elle	Steel Fixer
Oprea	Laurentiu	SRM	Labourer
Otuedon	Kingsley	London Tower Crane	Crane operator
Paladi	Sandor	ESL	Landscaping
Palliser	James	Heritage Brickwork	Foreman
Panton	Carlos	Access Solutions	Scaffolder
Parker	Billy	Access Solutions	Scaffolder
Pasaila	Adrian	Corbyn	Concrete Finisher
Paschalis	Levantazis	Corbyn	Groundworker
Patel	Sarjay	Osborne	Design Manager
Pawel	Klos	TRT	Installer
Peakin	Jeremy	LB of Southwark	Project Manager

Surname	First name	Company	Trade
Pearce	Zen	Britelec	Data Engineer
Penn	Luke	D & R	Steel erector
Perkins	Anthony	Osborne	Quantity Surveyor
Petkov	Galin	Rossoguil	Tape & Jointing
Petreseu	Isaia	Corbyn	Carpenter
Petutla-Alima	Roman	CPS Cleaning Ltd	Cleaning
Pietrasiak	Marcin	TRT	Installer
Pietrzykowska	A	Osborne	Surveyor
Piniuc	Romeo	Corbyn	Supervisor
Piniuc	Vasile	Corbyn	Carpenter
Pjetri	Nue		
Platts	Steve	LB of Southwark	Regeneration
Popescu	Marius	Corbyn	Steel Fixer
Popov	Vasil	SRM	
Potter	E	Jackson Drilling	Driller
Potter	Liam	D & R	Steel erector
Prescott	Alfie	Access Solutions	Labourer
Profir	Daniel	AC Beck & Sons	Painter
Pungut	Gesa	EWS	Window fixer
Pyzewski	Sebastian	Trott	Fixer
Quinn	Tony	Propak	Fixer
Radev	Rumen	NHE	Carpenter
Raducanu	Petru	AC Beck & Sons	Painter
Randell	Andrew	Access Solutions	Supervisor
Reed	Neil	Van Elle	Piler
Reeves	Gregory	WFP	Surveyor
Regan	Chris	Access Solutions	Scaffolder
Regan	Stephen	Access Solutions	Scaffolder
Regan	Jack	Access Solutions	Scaffolder

Surname	First name	Company	Trade
Rendall-Moniz	Vitor	S R McHugh	Labourer
Roberts	James	WFP	Engineer
Roe	Jon	Access Solutions	Scaffolder
Rogojan	Nicolae	EWS	Fixer
Rowlett	L	D & R	Steel erector
Royan	Aldier	Heritage Brickwork	Labourer
Ruci	Xhevdet	Corbyn	Steel Fixer
Rudzinski	Kamil	Houton Construction Services	Carpenter
Rusu	Crisoihel	Corbyn	Traffic Banksman
Ryan	Christopher	D & R	Fabrication Welder
Ryan	John	Corbyn	Groundworker
Ryszawy	Kristian	London Wall	Installer
Saks	Priit	London Wall	Labourer
Samuda	Patrick	Trott	Labourer
Sandu	Viorel	Corbyn	Concrete Finisher
Sargent	Daren	D & R	Steel erector
Saunders	Nigel	Trott	Ceiling fixer
Sava	Mariana	CPS Cleaning Ltd	Cleaning
Saxton	Mike	Osborne	Site Manager
Schepes	Paul	Sorba	Surveyor
Scott	Simeon		Visitor
Selmane	A	Constructive Resource	Crane operator
Sharrock	Paul	Thomas Ford & Partners	Surveyor
Sheens	Steve	Van Elle	Piler
Shegaj	A	Corbyn	Groundworker

Surname	First name	Company	Trade
Shehu	Isa	Corbyn	Steel Fixer
Sheremetov	Chardar	Trott	Fixer
Shield	Elvon	AC Beck & Sons	Painter
Simmons	Terry	Access Solutions	Scaffolder
Singh	Majinder	S R McHugh	Crane Supervisor
Singh	Mandeep	Corbyn	Concrete Finisher
Singh	Awinder	Corbyn	Concrete Finisher
Singh	Jasvir	Corbyn	Concrete Finisher
Singh	A	Heritage Brickwork	Labourer
Singh	Amarjeet	SRM	Labourer
Siveri	Giorgo	AC Beck & Sons	Painter
Smedley	Connor	Ecolutions	Solar Electrician
Smith	J		Visitor
Smith	Gary	Propak	Glazing
Smith	James	MWC Roofing	Roofer
Smythe	Neil		Visitor
Smythe	Neil	AC Projects	Lagger
Snihur	Nazar	Heritage Brickwork	Handyman
Soro	David	van Heyningen and Haward	Architect
Stanila	Serghei	Heritage Brickwork	Bricklayer
Stansfield	Alex	FST	Fire Protection
Steele	C	Floorcraft	Floorlayer
Stephen	Ian	Dyson Briggs	Tiler
Stocker	Kevin	AC Projects	Fitter
Stoian	Stefan	SRM	Plant operator
Stowell	Kemsley	Shire	Carpenter
Stratan	Serghei	MWC Roofing	Roofer
Stratulat	Dimitru	MWC Roofing	Roofer

Surname	First name	Company	Trade
Suleiman	Adam	Casi	Kitchen Fitter
Suliman	G	S R McHugh	Labourer
Sulinan	S	S R McHugh	Labourer
Supe	Janis	Corbyn	Groundworker
Surau	Ionica	Corbyn	Groundworks
Sweeney	Shane	Access Solutions	Scaffolder
Symons	Anthony	Heritage Brickwork	Bricklayer
Tabat	Patryk	Corbyn	Steel Fixer
Tandon	Rohan	Corbyn	Concrete Finisher
Tanner	Terry	Jackson Drilling	Driller
Tanoveanu	Mihai	AC Beck & Sons	Painter
Taoself	Creon	Mott MacDonald	Project Manager
Tarba	Vasile	EWS	Window fixer
Taylor	Dean	AC Projects	Electrician
Terry	Courtney	Access Solutions	Scaffolder
Thomas	Jared	King Lifting	Tower Crane Op
Thomas	G	S R McHugh	Labourer
Thomas	A	Guideline	Lift engineer
Thompson	Leon		Visitor
Thurlow	David	Access Solutions	Scaffolder
Tiper	Victor	Corbyn	Groundworker
Tomaszek	Tomasz	TRT	Manager
Torvinen	Rami	London Wall	Labourer
Traian	Constantin	Corbyn	Carpenter
Triolo	Thomson	Corbyn	Groundworker
Turta	Costanel	Corbyn	Steel Fixer
Udugba	G	Sorba	Project Manager
Ungureanu	Bogdan	Corbyn	Steel Fixer
Usher	Ross	A & K Services	Plumber

Surname	First name	Company	Trade
Valentine	Geoff		Clerk of Works
Van Der Westhuizen	D	London Tower Crane	Electrician
Vasileiou	Andreas	Corbyn	Steel Fixer
Vennall	Daniel	Prodeck	Steel erector
Verban	Petrica	Corbyn	Labourer
Verstiuc	Denis	MWC Roofing	Roofer
Vidler	Richard	London Tower Crane	Electrician
Vidrascu	Constantin	AC Beck & Sons	Painter
Vinogradous	Igors	Corbyn	Steel Fixer
Waghorn	Max	C & S Erections	Ductwork fitter
Waghorn	Brian	C & S Erections	Ductwork fitter
Wale	M	NHE	Carpenter
Wale	Mark	NHE	Carpenter
Walls	James	Floorcraft	Floorlayer
Ward	S	AC Projects	Ductwork fitter
Ward	J	ARC Controls	Engineer
Watson	Colin	CETCo	Surveyor
Watson	Connor	Access Solutions	Labourer
Wheeler	S	Heritage Brickwork	Bricklayer
White	Russell	Propak	Fixer
Whittley	M	Access Solutions	Scaffolder
Wicken	Alex	Access Solutions	Scaffolder
Wickwar	Richard	D & R	Steel erector
Wilkins	Damian	M+H Testing	Tester
Williams	Mark	LB of Southwark	Councillor
Williams	Stevie	Access Solutions	Labourer
Williams	Mavin	Heritage Brickwork	Labourer
Wilson	Jonathan	ESD	

Surname	First name	Company	Trade
Wixon	Mick	AC Projects	Insulation
Wlosek	Miwal	FST	Painter
Wlosek	Siawislaw	FST	Painter
Wood	Dan	D & R	Steel erector
Woronowicz	Piotr	Trott	Jointer
York	Brian	Propak	Glazing
Young	David	D & R	Driller
Young	Cameron	D & R	Driller
Zmurda	Adam	Trott	Tape & Jointing

APPENDIX II

Members of Crossway United Reformed Church as at 1st April 2018

Josephine Adeoye		Edward Kyere	
Marcia Ayala		Valerie McDonald	
James Boye		Daniel Oppong	
Christal Bratley	*Treasurer*	Felix Osei	
Mandy Buckberry	*GB Captain*	Emmanuel Osei-Somuah	*Elder*
Russell Buckberry	*GB Lieutenant*	Ruby Osekreh	
BB Cobbinah	*Elder*	Adelaide Owusu	*Elder*
Ian Coll		Erica Owusu	
Paulina Coll		Regina Owusu-Agyirifo	
Amah Deinde		Stephenie Robinson	*Elder*
Tobi Deinde		Sally Skaife	*Elder*
Hadji Diallo		Peter Stevenson	
Eric Gyamfi	*Elder*	Rachel St Clair	*Elder*
Fernanda Herrera		Fumi St Marthe	
George Jackson		John St Marthe	
Edwin Jarrin		Eric Dollar Tuffour-Frempong	
Elizabeth Kobreni			

Appendix III

User Groups at Crossway Christian Centre as at 31st March 2018

Be Enriched Castle Canteen	Social enterprise offering free lunches
Glory Church	French-speaking African prayer group
The Motivational Centre	Congregation for people with a disability
Robes Project	Day care for homeless people
Resurrection Power of Christ	English-speaking African Charismatic Sunday church
ADUK-MC	Portuguese-speaking Brazilian congregation
Akrofonso Kroye Kuo	Ghanaian community group
Cali Driving School	Spanish-speaking written drive test tuition
The Christian Community	Spanish-speaking Charismatic church
Emmaus Church	Spanish-speaking Charismatic church
Elephant and Castle Street Pastors	
Nick Blackburn	Freelance counsellor
Ghanaian Presbyterian Church	
Michelle Harrison	Ballet lessons for children and adults

International Apostolic Ministries	Spanish-speaking apostolic church
Christ Victorious	Prayer group
Gospel Ministry International Church	Ethiopian/Eritrean women's prayer group
Housing Action Southwark and Lambeth	Spanish-speaking housing advice group
Pan & Tortas Ezekiel 4:9	Healthy food with biblical input
More than Blessed	Prayer and cell group of Spanish church
Royal Faith Ministries	Ghanaian prayer group
Lambeth Reborn	Youth adult worship group
Reach Out from the King's Altar	Prayer group
Prophetic Praise Healing Ministries	Independent worship group

Contact Crossway

To contact Crossway, please send an email to:

revdpete@btinternet.com

More information about the church can be found on the web page:

www.crosswaychurch.org.uk

Related Books by the Publisher

Hope in the Main Street
Rob Cotton

Rev. Rob Cotton demonstrates how our churches can engage with the community around, building relationships that enable social action, presenting the teachings of the Bible in ways that contemporary audiences can relate to and presenting Christianity as genuine good news.

Rob has led a number of churches, as well as being Senior Campaign Manager at Bible Society and on the leadership teams for national campaigns such as Hope 08, Biblefresh and The 2011 Trust (celebrating the 400th anniversary of the King James Bible). From the humorous to the heartbreaking, these stories from his years of ministry will equip you, encourage you and challenge you to bring 'hope on the main street'.

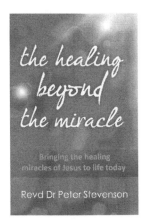

The Healing Beyond the Miracle
Revd Dr Peter Stevenson

The Bible is our spiritual food – daily bread that can help us live in relationship with Jesus and in accordance with God's perfect plan. But for many of us the stories of scripture can be difficult to fully understand. They are translated from another language, another culture, another time. Without significant academic training, how can today's believer enjoy the inner nourishment that scripture is supposed to provide?

Revd Dr Peter Stevenson provides us with a fresh way to bring the Bible stories alive, using the healing miracles of Jesus as examples. He invites us to seek out the healing beyond the miracle, the hidden voices of the many onlookers who were impacted by Jesus' ministry.

Available from all good bookshops and *www.onwardsandupwards.org*.